EXODUS

EXODUS

by
RONALD F. YOUNGBLOOD

MOODY PRESS
CHICAGO

All Scripture quotations in this book, except those identified otherwise, are from the
New International Version of the Holy Bible, © 1978 by New York International Bible
Society, and are used by permission.

Library of Congress Cataloging in Publication Data

Youngblood, Ronald F.
  Exodus.

  1. Bible. O.T. Exodus—Criticism, interpretation,
etc. I. Title.
BS1245.2.Y68 1983   222'.1207   82-21709
ISBN 0-8024-2002-8

2 3 4 5 6 7 Printing/LC/Year 88 87 86 85 84

Printed in the United States of America

CONTENTS

PREFACE

Any one of a half dozen books could easily lay claim to being the greatest and most important in the Old Testament. Genesis would get quite a number of votes because it describes the beginning of heaven and earth, of man and the animals, of love and marriage, of sin and salvation, and much more. Deuteronomy, a magnificent sermon right from the heart of Moses, is the favorite of many because of its beautiful summary of the gracious compassion of a covenant-making God toward His often rebellious people. So popular are the Psalms, the marvelous collection of hymns that have stirred the souls of believers down through the ages, that they are often appended to our New Testaments. Isaiah finds its advocates because of its unparalleled descriptions of the nature and attributes of God as well as its frequent predictions of the coming of the Messiah. Jeremiah is loved by others because of its lengthy reflections on what it cost to be God's prophet during the invasion of Jerusalem and destruction of the Temple by a ruthless Babylonian king. Daniel also attracts considerable attention because of its remarkably detailed prophecies of future events leading up to the first advent of Jesus Christ centuries later.

When all is said and done, however, I am becoming increasingly convinced that Exodus is the Old Testament's greatest book. Not only does it expand on many of the themes and bring to fruition many of the promises of Genesis, but it also introduces us to the most profound meanings of the Lord's name, to the most basic summary of the Lord's law, to the divine instructions that brought into being the Lord's Tabernacle and priesthood, and to the divine initiative that established the Lord's covenant—the old covenant, the covenant that gives our Old Testament its very name.

But there is more. The book of Exodus tells us about the miraculous redemption of the Israelites from their Egyptian slavemasters. The glorious truth that God brought His people "out of Egypt, out of the land of slavery" (Exod. 20:2) rings like a refrain throughout the rest of the Old Testament. The story of Exodus is the story of how God redeemed His own.

The commentary in the following pages is arranged in topical order and for the most part in the chapter sequence of Exodus itself. It is divided into thirteen sections to facilitate its use as a manual for weekly Bible or Sunday school classes over the course of a quarter.

1

INTRODUCTION

My first trip to the Holy Land took place in 1964, and our excitement was almost unbearable as we completed the next-to-last leg of our transatlantic flight and stepped off the plane in Athens for a brief refueling stop. After an hour or so in the terminal we heard our flight announced over the loudspeaker, and we began walking through the transit lounge back to the plane outside. Just as we arrived at the door leading out of the terminal building, my attention was drawn to a sign in Greek letters over the doorway. It read: EXODOS.

EXODOS—that was the name given by early Greek translators to the book we are studying. It means "exit," "road out," "way out," "departure" and is translated "exodus" in Hebrews 11:22 and "departure" in Luke 9:31 (it appears also in the Greek translation of Exod. 19:1). Our English word *exodus* is simply the Latin form of the Greek word and has come to us from Jerome's Latin translation of the Bible, known as the Vulgate.

The original Hebrew title of the book follows the common ancient practice of naming a book after its first few words—in this case "And these are the names of." The same phrase occurs in Genesis 46:8, and there it also introduces a list of the names of the Israelites "who entered Egypt with Jacob" (Exod. 1:1). The Hebrew title of the book of Exodus, therefore, serves to remind us that Exodus is the sequel to Genesis and that one of its purposes is to continue the history of

God's people as well as to elaborate further on the great themes so nobly introduced in Genesis.

AUTHOR OF THE BOOK

Unlike Genesis, which is anonymous as far as internal evidence is concerned (although Jewish and Christian tradition agree that it was written by Moses and therefore call it "The First Book of Moses"), Exodus claims in more than one place that Moses wrote at least substantial sections of it. Moses was told to write on a scroll the story of the Israelite victory over the Amalekites (Exod. 17:14). Elsewhere we learn that he "wrote down everything the LORD had said" (24:4), probably including at least 20:18—23:33, a law code known as "the Book of the Covenant" (24:7). The Lord also told Moses to write down the Ten Commandments, this time on two stone tablets (34:4, 27-29). As if to confirm Mosaic authorship of those legal sections, Mark 7:10 attributes one of the commandments (Exod. 20:12) and a verse from the Book of the Covenant (21:17) to Moses. In addition, Mark 12:26 states that Exodus 3:6 is found in "the book of Moses" (see also Luke 20:37), and Luke 2:22-23 quotes Exodus 13:2, 12 from a volume entitled alternately "the Law of Moses" and "the Law of the Lord." In so doing, Luke asserts his belief in the divine inspiration of the book of Exodus as well.

For the past hundred years or so it has been fashionable in some circles to attribute the authorship of Exodus to three anonymous writers known respectively by the initials "J" (for "Jahvist" or "Yahwist" after the divine name *Yahweh,* translated conventionally as "LORD"), "E" (for "Elohist" after the divine name *Elohim,* the Hebrew word for "God"), and "P" (for "priestly"). The first, said to have done his work in the tenth or ninth century B.C., is presumed to have preferred the intimate and personal name *Yahweh* in reference to God. On the other hand the so-called "Elohist" writer, who is supposed to have lived in the ninth or eighth century, is said to have preferred the more general term

Elohim. (We are also told by the proponents of this "documentary" theory, as it is called, that the "Yahwist" lived in Judah, the Southern Kingdom, whereas the "Elohist" was from the Northern Kingdom, known as both Israel and Ephraim. Thus "J" can stand for either "Jahvist" or "Judah," and "E" can stand for either "Elohist" or "Ephraim.") The "priestly" writer is so named because he is said to have been unusually interested in matters related to Israel's priesthood, such as laws, sacrifices, rituals, ceremonies, genealogies, and the like. His work is assumed to have been done in the sixth century B.C. or later. It is finally proposed that an even later editor, or compiler, gathered together the writings of "J," "E," and "P" and interwove them to form our present book of Exodus, this latter process taking place centuries after the time of Moses.

The combination of internal biblical evidence (both Old Testament and New) and unanimous Judeo-Christian tradition, however, provides conclusive evidence in favor of Mosaic authorship as opposed to the anonymous writers that the documentary hypothesis suggests. Diversity within the book of Exodus can just as easily be explained by noting the differences in theme and subject matter found there as it can by positing a different writer for each theme. The same writer—if he is competent—will vary his pace, his style, his vocabulary as his themes change. On the other hand, the unity of the book of Exodus is better explained by attributing the entire work to one writer—Moses—than to several (a problem tacitly admitted by proponents of "J," "E," and "P" when they are forced to create an "editor" to unify the various "documents" at the end of the process).

Moses himself, then, remains the best candidate for the authorship of Exodus. Moses had the necessary education, having been raised by his Hebrew mother during his earliest years and later having been adopted by the daughter of the Egyptian pharaoh himself (Exod. 2:8-10), in whose court he received his formal schooling (see Acts 7:22). Moses had the necessary incentive, since he is the main character in the story of the Exodus as the one who, under divine impulse and direction, led his fellow Israelites out of slavery in Egypt and to the borders of the Promised Land. Moses had the necessary time, since it took him and his people forty years to complete their desert journey. In short, Moses had every possible qualification needed to enable him to write a book like Exodus.

DATE OF THE BOOK

Moses could not have begun writing Exodus much before his eightieth year (Exod. 7:7), which coincided with the rapidly moving events that led up to the Exodus itself. If it is possible, then, to determine the date of the Exodus, the period when Moses composed the book of Exodus will be roughly the same as the period during which the Israelites were making their way through the Sinai desert. Although many dates for the Exodus have been proposed, the two dominant views place it either in the eighteenth Egyptian dynasty (the so-called "early date" theory) on the one hand or the nineteenth dynasty (the so-called "late date" theory) on the other.

The main argument used in favor of a nineteenth dynasty date is the statement in Exodus 1:11 that the Israelites were forced to build "Pithom and Rameses as store cities for Pharaoh." Ramses II, one of the most ambitious builders of all time, is known both historically and archaeologically to have constructed a number of royal residence cities in the delta region, Pithom and Rameses being just two of them. Assuming that Exodus 1:11 refers to their original founding under Ramses, those who hold to the late date have placed the Exodus at about 1295 or 1290 B.C. and have made Seti I (founder of the nineteenth dynasty) the pharaoh of the oppression and his son Ramses II the pharaoh of the Exodus itself.

Additional arguments are also proposed in support of a nineteenth dynasty date. First Kings 6:1 refers to "the fourth year of Solomon's reign over Israel" (that is, 966 B.C.) as "the four hundred and eightieth year after the Israelites had come out of Egypt.'' The proponents of the ''late date'' theory suggest that the figure *480* is a round number for twelve generations of a symbolic 40 years apiece and that, since 25 years is a more normal and realistic estimate for the typical generation (that is, the age of a man when he fathers his firstborn son), the 480 of 1 Kings 6:1 really means approximately 300 in terms of actual calendar years. Adding 300 to 966 B.C. dates the Exodus at about 1266 B.C., close enough to the 1290 date mentioned earlier and well within the time span of the long reign of Ramses II. It is also noted that Merneptah, Ramses' son and successor, left a monument in his mortuary temple at Thebes in southern Egypt that refers to Israel as living in Canaan in an unsettled condition, possibly a description of their situation before they had finished conquering the Promised Land.

Other reasons for dating the Exodus relatively late tend to be based on archaeological research, such as indications of numerous Canaanite towns having been destroyed in the late thirteenth century B.C. (presumably by the invading Israelites) and of almost complete lack of settled populations east of the Jordan river and south of the Dead Sea until the thirteenth century (thus providing no Edomite or Moabite opposition to the Israelites—although the Bible states that there was in fact such opposition—earlier than that time).

The ''early date'' theorists, meanwhile, say that there is no compelling reason to understand the 480 years of 1 Kings 6:1 in any way other than literal. Adding 480 to 966 B.C. dates the Exodus at about 1445 B.C., making Thutmose III the pharaoh of the oppression and Amunhotep II the pharaoh of the Exodus itself. Those who hold to the early date then go on to point out that the Exodus 1:11 reference to ''Rameses'' no more dates the Exodus during the reign of Ramses II than the reference to ''the district of Rameses'' in Genesis 47:11 dates the time of Joseph (to which that verse refers) during the reign of Ramses II. In both Genesis and Exodus, ''Rameses'' was not the original name of the site but represents a minor editorial change made by scribes long after Moses' time to update the references for their readers, just as "Dan" in Genesis 14:14 is an editorial update for the name of a city that was called "Laish" until the days of the judges (Judg. 18:29).

As for the Merneptah monument, the unsettled condition of the Israelites in the late thirteenth century can describe their situation at some periods during the days of the judges just as easily as at the time of the conquest. The archaeological information concerning the destruction of Canaanite towns late in the thirteenth century also fits the period of the judges if the "early date" theory be held. And recent archaeological investigation has shown that the Edomite and Moabite homelands were in fact far more heavily populated before the thirteenth century than had formerly been thought, so that fifteenth-century Israelites would indeed have met strong resistance when they requested permission to pass through those territories.

To summarize, then, no longer are there weighty reasons for preferring the 1295 date over the 1445 date. Indeed, there are powerful additional reasons for preferring the earlier date over the later—reasons to which we now turn.

"During that long period, the king of Egypt died" (Exod. 2:23). Thutmose III, the pharaoh of the oppression according to the "early date" theory, had a long reign (about 1490-1436 B.C.), whereas Seti I, his counterpart according to the "late date" theory, ruled for a much shorter period. Or again: "Every firstborn son in Egypt will die, from the firstborn son of Pharaoh, who sits on the throne, to the firstborn son of the slave girl" (Exod. 11:5). As far as we know, Merneptah was Ramses's firstborn son and, since he succeeded his father as pharaoh, he did not die from the tenth plague. The firstborn son of Amunhotep II, however, died before his father did, since Thutmose IV, a younger son of Amunhotep, succeeded him as pharaoh. It is therefore possible that Amunhotep's firstborn was struck dead by the Lord during the night of the tenth plague.

The earth sciences have recently come to the aid of the

"early date" theory as well. Whatever one might think in general of the hypotheses of Immanuel Velikovsky, the writer of best-sellers *Worlds in Collision, Ages in Chaos,* and *Earth in Upheaval,* he has at least forced scientists to seriously consider the possibility that in the fifteenth century B.C. earth-shaking events of cosmic significance (perhaps precipitating the plagues that led to the Exodus?) took place all over the world. One such occurrence was a fiery volcanic eruption of unprecedented violence that took place during the fifteenth century B.C. on the Aegean island of Santorini (about seventy miles north of Crete), confirmed in 1956 by Angelos Galanopoulos of the Athens Seismological Institute.[1]

Galanopoulos connects the eruption and its resulting tidal waves to the sudden disappearance of the ancient Minoan civilization as well as to the account of the Athenian lawgiver Solon concerning the destruction of the legendary island of Atlantis. Others have related the Santorini explosion to the ten plagues in Exodus, whereas Galanopoulos himself believes that its tidal waves drowned the pharaoh's armies as they pursued the Israelites, who were crossing the Sea of Reeds (Exod. 14:26-28). At least one eminent Egyptologist, Hans Goedicke of Johns Hopkins University, agrees with Galanopoulos—although he differs with him concerning the location of the Sea and asserts (on the basis of a recently reinterpreted Egyptian text) that the pharaoh of the Exodus was Queen Hatshepsut and that the Exodus occurred in 1477 B.C.[2] (about thirty years earlier than the traditional date).

Goedicke's conclusions are being hotly debated at present, but enough has been said in the previous paragraph to in-

---

1. Angelos Galanopoulos and Edward Bacon, *Atlantis: The Truth Behind the Legend* (Indianapolis: Bobbs-Merrill, 1969). For a popular treatment see Ronald Schiller, "The Explosion That Changed the World," *Reader's Digest,* November 1967, pp. 122-27.
2. See provisionally John Noble Wilford, "Theory Ties Exodus Flood to Tidal Wave," *New York Times,* 4 May 1981, p. 1; Sharon Begley, "A Watered-Down Exodus," *Newsweek,* 18 May 1981, p. 131.

dicate that the fifteenth century B.C. provides a suitable physical environment for the phenomena leading up to and surrounding the Exodus event. (It goes without saying that miracles were involved, but we must always reckon with the possibility that God many use secondary means even as He performs miracles.)

A final bit of evidence may be derived from the recently discovered Ebla tablets at Tell Mardikh in northern Syria, a find that is forcing Bible scholars of the caliber of David Noel Freedman to consider pushing the date of Abraham back to a much earlier period.[3] That in turn, of course, makes the earlier date of the Exodus more attractive since the book of Exodus itself gives 430 years as the length of time from the migration of Jacob's family into Egypt (Exod. 1:1) to the release of his descendants from slavery there (12:40-41).

Although, as one distinguished researcher puts it, "the problem is extremely complex,"[4] the available evidence once again seems to be tilting rather decisively in favor of the traditional date of the Exodus—about 1445 B.C. The following commentary will therefore take for granted the strong likelihood of the date proposed by the "early date" theory while at the same time making no claims to omniscience concerning this difficult matter.

Outline of the Book

The book of Exodus divides rather naturally into three main sections, the first and third of which portray Israel in a stationary position (in Egypt and at Sinai respectively), whereas the central section (the heart of the book) describes Israel on the move (from Egypt to Sinai). The following outline attempts to represent the threefold division (with its major subdivisions).

---

3. See, for example, David Noel Freedman, "The Real Story of the Ebla Tablets," *Biblical Archaeologist* 41 (December 1978): 143-64.
4. H. H. Rowley, *From Joseph to Joshua* (Oxford: U. Press, 1950), p. 12.

THEME OF THE BOOK

The establishment of God's chosen people of Israel as "a kingdom of priests and a holy nation" (Exod. 19:6) is the major theme of the book of Exodus. The story is here told of how God fulfilled one of His promises to Abraham by making him "very fruitful" (Gen. 17:6; see Exod. 1:7), how God freed Israel from Egyptian slavery, how God renewed the Abrahamic covenant with them at Mount Sinai, and how God provided them with rules for life and worship. The story of Exodus is the story of how God redeemed His people.

2

PERSECUTION

I. ISRAEL IN EGYPT: SLAVERY (1:1—12:30)

Egypt is the locale of the last verse of Genesis as well as of
the first verse of Exodus. The last fourteen chapters of
Genesis tell the exciting story of the migration of Jacob, his
sons, and their families into Egypt, and the first twelve
chapters of Exodus tell the equally dramatic story of how a
change of power in Egypt (Exod. 1:8) produced a series of
pharaohs who enslaved Jacob's descendants and who, in so
doing, were then brought into direct conflict with the God
who redeems.

The ancient Greek historian Herodotus aptly described
Egypt as "the gift of the Nile." Lacking the life-giving waters
of the Nile, Egypt would never have been able to develop into
one of the most powerful and sophisticated civilizations of
the ancient world. A green gash of water that cuts through
one of the most arid deserts on earth, the river consists of the
White Nile, with its source in Uganda, and the Blue Nile, with
its source in modern Ethiopia. The two Niles become one at
Khartoum, the capital of modern Sudan, but it is the waters
of the Blue Nile that cause the annual flooding that produces
the remarkable fertility of soil characteristic of the main river
valley. The 550 miles of territory from Khartoum north to
Aswan (see Ezek. 29:10; 30:6) constituted ancient Nubia (the
Old Testament "Cush"; see, for example, Isa. 18). The 500
miles from Aswan north to Memphis (Isa. 19:13; Jer. 2:16;
44:1; 46:14, 19; Ezek. 30:13, 16; Hos. 9:6) was Upper Egypt,

19

whereas the 100 miles from Memphis to the Mediterranean was Lower Egypt (the delta region, including Goshen).

The concept of Upper and Lower Egypt translated into Hebrew as *Mizraim* (see Gen. 10:6, 13), literally "two Egypts" but traditionally rendered simply as "Egypt." Although the first twelve chapters of Exodus are concerned only with Lower Egypt (the northern, or delta, region of the country), a brief historical sketch of the entire land will serve us well as background for a study of the book.

Manetho, an Egyptian priest who lived in the early third century B.C., divided the history of his people into thirty or thirty-one dynasties in a book entitled *Aigyptiaka hypomnēmata*. His basic pattern has been further nuanced into several distinct periods by modern scholars as follows: Dynasties 1-2, Early Dynastic; 3-8, Old Kingdom (Pyramid); 9-11, First Intermediate; 12-13, Middle Kingdom; 14-17, Second Intermediate; 18-20, New Kingdom (Empire); 21-25, Third Intermediate; 26, Saite; 27-30/31, Late Dynastic.

Writing was already in widespread use in Eygpt in the late fourth millennium B.C., when the first dynasty began. That writing in its various forms yielded to decipherment through the brilliant work of the French scholar Champollion in 1822, when he managed to read a lengthy trilingual inscription that had been found by Napoleon's army near the Rosetta mouth of the Nile on the Mediterranean two decades earlier. Champollion's research opened the way for our modern understanding of ancient Egyptian history and culture.

The history of ancient Egypt is often the story of a powerful ruler from Upper Egypt conquering the north and unifying the country. Narmer, the first significant ruler of the Early Dynastic period (about 3100-2686 B.C.), united the crown of Upper Egypt (a tall white helmet) with that of Lower Egypt (a red wickerwork diadem). No other kings of his reputation or stature emerged in Egypt until the Old Kingdom period (about 2686-2160 B.C.).

The Pyramid Age (especially Dynasties 3-6) constituted a

time during which Egypt was doubtless the world's major civilization. Its pharaohs were considered by their people and by themselves to be gods, who administered Egypt according to the overall principle of *maat* ("order," "justice," "truth"). Since by definition the king acted according to *maat* and therefore could do no wrong, he was the very embodiment of justice, making laws external to himself unnecessary. The Pyramid Age pharaohs and their successors were probably the most absolute monarchs the world has ever known and were believed to possess all the wisdom and power that deity normally commands. The titanic spiritual struggle that takes place between the one true God and the pharaohs of Egypt in Exodus 1:1—12:30 can best be understood against that backdrop.

Nearly eighty Egyptian pyramids have been identified, all of them witnesses to a strong belief in life after death. They are shaped like the sun's rays, the ramp or staircase on which the pharaoh ascended symbolically to the sun-god in heaven. Every pyramid was built on the desert sands west of the Nile, since west is the direction of the setting sun, the place of darkness, and since the desert is the dry land and therefore the realm of death. For that reason also the royal sarcophagus was always placed at the western end of the burial chamber inside the pyramid.

Zoser, an early ruler in Dynasty 3, had a remarkable stepped pyramid built for himself at Sakkarah, just south of Cairo and west of Memphis. The earliest tomb in pyramidal form and the oldest free-standing monumental structure on the earth's surface, it is 195 feet high.

Dynasty 4 (about 2613-2494 B.C.), however, represents the highwater mark of the Pyramid Age. Its second pharaoh, Khufu (called Cheops by the Greeks), built the greatest of all the pyramids, this time at Gizeh near Cairo. The third largest building in the modern world, it is the only surviving wonder of the Seven Wonders of the Ancient World. The largest tomb ever built, the pyramid of Cheops is 756 feet on a side,

450 feet high (481 feet originally), and covers thirteen acres. Well over two million stones, weighing from two-and-a-half to fifteen tons apiece, were used in its construction. According to Herodotus it took a hundred thousand men twenty years to build it.

The second ruler after Khufu was Khafre (Chephren), whose pyramid, still retaining its limestone cap, is the second largest of the pyramids (708 feet on a side, 466 feet high). Near its valley temple is the famous Sphinx (185 feet long, 65 feet high), carved out of a sandstone spur rising from the desert. Its face represents that of Chephren himself. Dynasty 6 (about 2345-2181 B.C.) is famous for the durable Pharaoh Pepi II, who ruled for about ninety years and therefore boasts the longest reign in recorded history.

The most important ruler of the First Intermediate period (about 2160-1991 B.C.) was Mentuhotep II, who moved the capital to Thebes in Upper Egypt. Located 440 miles south of Memphis (the capital of the Old Kingdom pharaohs) and destined much later to become Egypt's greatest capital, Thebes is called *No* (Egyptian for "The City Par Excellence") in Jeremiah 46:25 and Ezekiel 30:14-16, and *No-Amon* ("The City of the God Amun") in Nahum 3:8.

Amunemhet I, a Theban by birth whose very name signalizes the ascendancy of Amun, the god of Thebes, to supremacy in the Egyptian pantheon, founded the twelfth dynasty by becoming pharaoh of Upper and Lower Egypt with his royal residence at a city south of Memphis. In so doing he inaugurated the glorious Middle Kingdom period (which began in 1991 B.C., the earliest precise year-date in world history), the Egyptian "golden age," the apex of the civilization and culture of ancient Egypt. Amunemhet and his successors conquered lower Nubia, built a canal from the Nile to the Red Sea, and developed the Sinai turquoise mines into a permanent industry. The sixth year of Sesostris II (1892 B.C.) is the date of a famous wall painting in the tomb of a nobleman at Beni Hasan, 168 miles south of Cairo. It pictures a donkey caravan of thirty-seven Asiatics bringing goods to Egypt in a scene strikingly reminiscent of Genesis 45:20-22. By the time of Sesostris III (1878-1843 B.C.), however, hostilities between Egypt and the Asiatic Semites had grown to such an extent that the Egyptians began to compose curses against their enemies and inscribe them on pottery vessels and crude statuettes, later smashing them in acts of sympathetic magic akin to voodoo. It is all the more remarkable, therefore, that Joseph, himself an Asiatic Semite, found favor in the eyes of Sesostris III (see Gen. 41:39-45), who was probably the pharaoh when Joseph was sold into slavery in Egypt. Surely God was with Joseph in an unusual way (Gen. 39:2-3, 21, 23; 49:25; Acts 7:9) during that tense period of Egyptian history.

Stress and strain characterized the Second Intermediate period as well, especially during Dynasties 15-16 when the Asiatic Hyksos controlled Egypt. Under a general named Salitis, the Hyksos (Egyptian for "chiefs of foreign lands") invaded Egypt and set up their capital at Tanis (called Zoan in Num. 13:22; Ps. 78:12, 43) in the southeast delta region (the biblical Goshen). One of the secrets of the Hyksos' strength was their introduction of the horse and chariot into warfare. The Egyptians learned quickly, however, and two brothers, Kamose (the last ruler of Dynasty 17) and Ahmose (the first ruler of the New Kingdom and Dynasty 18), defeated the Hyksos and expelled them from the land of the Nile. The days of Egypt's imperial glory had begun.

If the Old Kingdom represented the age of absolute power for Egypt's pharaohs (exemplified by their magnificent pyramids), and if the Middle Kingdom represented the high-water mark of Egypt's culture and civilization (illustrated by its remarkable literary productions and artistic achievements), the New Kingdom represents Egypt at the zenith of her imperial might. The period was composed of Dynasties 18-20 and lasted for nearly half a millennium (about 1558-1085 B.C.). From Tanis in the delta to modern El-Kenisa in Sudan, monuments to Egypt's imperial glory can still be seen, and they provide a wealth of information about every aspect of Egyptian life and culture during those days.

The pharaohs of Dynasty 18 (about 1558-1303 B.C.) ruled for more than half of the New Kingdom period. The second ruler after Ahmose was his son-in-law Thutmose I, whose military campaigns ranged from the Euphrates in the northeast to Nubia in the south. Thutmose II, his son and successor, ruled only briefly. He in turn was succeeded by his sister, the remarkable Hatshepsut, who, in a man's world, had herself proclaimed "king" and affected male mannerisms including clothing and the false beard worn by her pharaonic predecessors. Her building efforts include the 350-ton obelisk (the tallest in Egypt) at Karnak (ancient Thebes). She was followed on the throne by her stepson, the great Thutmose III, who had nominally been co-regent during her reign. Thutmose attempted to obliterate the name and portrait of Hatshepsut wherever they appeared. He then turned his attention toward the conquest of Palestine, and in 1468 B.C. the name of the city of Megiddo emerged into prominence as Thutmose besieged and captured it in an attack that was as classic as it was brilliant. Plunder gained from his annual military campaigns made it possible for him to engage in large-scale building projects in Egypt. His massive obelisks, many of which have long since been removed from their original locations, can today be found in such remote cities as Istanbul, Rome, London, and New York. Egypt's empire was never more extensive than in the days of Thutmose III and his son Amunhotep II (probably the pharaoh of the oppression and the pharaoh of the Exodus respectively).

Amunhotep's son Thutmose IV recorded in his so-called Dream Inscription, located now on a red granite monument between the front paws of the Sphinx at Gizeh, that the sun god appeared to him and promised to make him the next pharaoh if he would clear away the drifting sands that were threatening to bury the Sphinx. Since the accession of Thutmose IV to the throne of Egypt would have been automatic if he was Amunhotep's firstborn son, it is obvious that one or more of Thutmose's older brothers would have to die before Thutmose himself could become pharaoh. It may well be, then, that an older brother of Thutmose IV was the pharaoh's son—that is, the firstborn of Amunhotep II—who died in the slaughter of the firstborn at the time of the tenth plague (Exod. 11:5; 12:29).

Our historical survey has now brought us to the general period of Egyptian history during which the events of the book of Exodus took place.

A. PHARAOH PERSECUTES ISRAEL (1:1-22)

Introduction (1:1-6). Exodus 1:6 reminds us that Joseph died, a fact mentioned in the last verse of Genesis. The introductory paragraph of Exodus therefore serves to tie the book closely to the one that precedes it and quickly summarizes the hundreds of years that have elapsed between Genesis 50:26 and Exodus 1:7.

Joseph's father was known as both "Jacob" and "Israel" (v. 1). "Jacob" means "He Grasps the Heel" (Gen. 25:26) or "He Deceives," as Jacob's brother, Esau, understood all too well (Gen. 27:36). But at the ford of the Jabbok Jacob's name was changed to "Israel," which means "He Struggles with God" and, by implication, overcomes (Gen. 32:28; see also 35:10). Jacob's descendants became known as Israelites, "Sons of the Overcomer," not as Jacobites, "Sons of the Deceiver," and it is as Israelites that they migrated to Egypt.

In verses 2-3 the sons of Leah (Reuben, Jacob's firstborn, through Zebulun), Jacob's first wife, are listed in the order of their birth. Then follows Benjamin, the younger son of Jacob's second wife, Rachel (her firstborn, Joseph, is not mentioned here because he was "already in Egypt"— v. 5—and the list includes only those "who entered Egypt with Jacob"—v. 1). Verse 4 then lists Dan and Naphtali, "the sons of Rachel's maidservant Bilhah" (Gen. 35:25), and Gad and Asher, "the sons of Leah's maidservant Zilpah" (Gen. 35:26). "Seventy" (v. 5) is the ideal and complete number of Jacob's descendants who would have gone to Egypt originally if Er and Onan had not died earlier. Their death in Canaan (Gen. 46:12) reduced the number to sixty-eight, and the birth of Joseph's sons, Manasseh and Ephraim, in Egypt (Gen. 46:20, 27) reduced the figure further to sixty-six (Gen. 46:26). The number "seventy-five" in Acts 7:14 probably includes additional descendants of Jacob (Joseph's younger children, for example) born after his arrival in Egypt.

The problem (1:7-10). Stephen tells us that the fruitfulness and increase of the Israelites noted in Exodus 1:7 was due to the fact that the time was near "for God to fulfill his promise to Abraham" (Acts 7:17). That promise, recorded in Genesis 17:2, 6 and 22:17, was built on a mandate given earlier to Adam (Gen. 1:28) and Noah (Gen. 9:1, 7) and was later confirmed to Abraham's son Isaac (Gen. 26:4) and his grandson Jacob (Gen. 28:14; 48:4). As verse 7 reminds us, the land (Goshen—see Gen. 45:10—in the southeast delta region) "was filled with them." Filled indeed—with 600,000 "men on foot, besides women and children" (Exod. 12:37)! From seventy all the way to between two and three million in just a few hundred years—God had truly multiplied His people.

But Israel's blessing became the pharaoh's problem. The "new king, who did not know about Joseph" (v. 8), was perhaps Ahmose (about 1558-1533 B.C.), who founded Dynasty 18 and expelled the Hyksos from Egypt. But whoever he was he did not want the Israelites to become so strong and numerous that they would be able to fight against Egypt and win their freedom.

The solution (1:11-22). The pharaoh's plan of oppression had three phases, each more ruthless than the preceding. First, he appointed slave masters to assemble Israelite work crews and "to oppress them with forced labor" (v. 11). The beating of a slave by such an overseer is vividly portrayed on a wall painting in the Theban tomb of Rekhmire (dated to the time of Thutmose III), and an associated inscription uses the Egyptian equivalent of the Hebrew word in verse 11 for "slave master" (*sār*). The exact locations of the store cities, Pithom and Rameses, are still debated. The word "pharaoh," Egyptian in origin and meaning "great house," is a royal title and not a personal name. Although the pharaoh's overseers made the Israelites' lives "bitter" (v. 14), a fact later commemorated in the Passover meal (Exod. 12:8), the descendants of Jacob continued to multiply and spread (v. 12).

The pharaoh then put into operation phase two of his plan (vv. 15-21). He told the Hebrew midwives to kill all the newborn male infants but to let the newborn girls live. Although the biblical term "Hebrew" is probably cognate to the similar word *'apiru* (found in Egyptian, Babylonian, and Canaanite texts), the latter was applied to a population element that was ethnically diverse and that had in common only a generally inferior social status. The word "Hebrew" is almost always used by Gentiles to distinguish Israelites ethnically from other peoples and apparently denotes descent from Eber (Gen. 10:24-25; 11:14-17), whose ancestor was Noah's son Shem (Gen. 10:21). "Shiphrah" and "Puah" were ancient Northwest Semitic feminine personal names, the former attested in an Egyptian list of Asiatic slaves from the period of Dynasty 13 and the latter occurring in a Canaanite religious text contemporary with Moses. Since the Israelites were so numerous, many other midwives probably assisted Shiphrah and Puah. The Hebrew term for "delivery stool" means literally "two stones," doubtless with a space between them (a woman would then sit on them while giving birth).

If the pharaoh's command to the midwives had been carried out, it would have been a master stroke. The fewer Israelite male infants, the smaller would have been the number of potential Israelite warriors, the smaller would have been the number of potential Israelite husbands to produce offspring, and the greater would have been the number of potential Israelite women for the king's harem. But the midwives "feared God" (v. 17) in the sense that they expressed reverential trust in Him by committing themselves to obey His will rather than that of the pharaoh (for a parallel in Israel's later history see Acts 5:29) and allowed the male babies to remain alive. Their excuse to the pharaoh was by no means completely truthful (v. 19), but God gave the midwives "families of their own" because of their determination to obey Him (v. 21). The end result was that the Israelites continued to grow in strength and numbers (v. 20).

Deceived and frustrated by the midwives, the pharaoh put the third and last phase of his sinister plan into operation: He ordered all his countrymen to throw every newborn Hebrew boy into the river (v. 22)—that is, the Nile (the word for "river" is the normal Egyptian term for "Nile"). Genocide, the killing off of an entire ethnic population, was the pharaoh's solution to his problem. In a chillingly similar modern situation, Adolph Hitler called the same procedure the "final solution."

3

PREPARATION

B. GOD PREPARES A LEADER (2:1—4:31)

The Lord's response to the pharaoh's murderous scheme was to raise up a man who would eventually lead the Israelites out of bondage and into freedom. That man was Moses, who is considered by many to be the greatest single individual in the entire Old Testament and who is the principal figure in the biblical narrative from Exodus 2 through the end of Deuteronomy.

1. *Moses' early life* (2:1-25). The boy's family came from the tribe of Levi (v. 1). We learn later that Moses' father and mother were named Amram and Jochebed, who was Amram's aunt (Exod. 6:20). Even as an infant, Moses' appearance and character were unusual, since he is referred to as "a fine child" (v. 2), "no ordinary child" (Acts 7:20; Heb. 11:23), "fair in the sight of God" (Acts 7:20, footnote). To save him from the pharaoh's wrath Jochebed put the baby in a "papyrus basket" and set it afloat in the Nile among the "reeds" (v. 3).

The Hebrew words translated "papyrus," "basket," and "reeds" are all of Egyptian derivation. Papyrus was used not only as a writing material but also to make large, seaworthy boats (Isa. 18:2), the forerunners of those that carried Thor Heyerdahl and his crew safely across the Atlantic several years ago during the two Ra expeditions. The word for "basket" is used only here and of Noah's "ark," which was

29

also coated with "pitch" (v. 3; Gen. 6:14) to make it water-tight. Both vessels saved the life of a man of God. The word for "reeds" recurs in the proper name "Sea of Reeds" (Exod. 10:19 and frequently).

The baby's older sister, whose name was Miriam (Num. 26:59), stood close enough to the Nile to see what would happen to him. The "Pharaoh's daughter" (v. 5) was perhaps the eighteenth dynasty princess who later became Queen Hatshepsut (about 1490-1469 B.C.). Seeing the infant in the basket, she felt sorry for him and was pleased when Miriam offered to find a Hebrew woman to nurse him. Miriam, of course, chose Jochebed for the task. And so it was that three women—the mother, the sister, the pharaoh's daughter—conspired to thwart the designs of an evil pharaoh. The women remain anonymous in Exodus 2, as if to stress the fact that God in His providence was working behind the scenes.

The boy himself, however, did not long remain anonymous. In due course the pharaoh's daughter adopted him and gave him the Egyptian name "Moses," a word that means "is born" and forms the second element in such contemporary pharaonic names as Ahmose, Kamose, and Thutmose. The phrase "drew him out" (v. 10) is a Hebrew pun on the name, emphasizing the baby's rescue from the waters of the Nile.

The next time we meet Moses he had already "grown up" (v. 11) and was now "forty years old" (Acts 7:23). He went out to watch the Israelite labor crews at work and saw a fellow Hebrew being cruelly beaten by an Egyptian. Later, when no one else was around, he killed the Egyptian and buried his body. The next day, while trying to break up a fight between two Hebrews, he discovered that his killing of the Egyptian had become known. Moses, therefore, had no choice but to flee the wrath of the "Pharaoh" (v. 15), probably Thutmose III.

Two New Testament passages reflect on this story.[1]

---

1. For additional details see Brevard S. Childs, *Biblical Theology in Crisis* (Philadelphia: Westminster, 1970), chap. 10.

Stephen tells us that when one of the two Hebrew fighters sarcastically asked Moses, "Who made you ruler and judge over us?" (v. 14), he was unwittingly making a prediction that would be fulfilled forty years later (Acts 7:27, 30, 35). The Hebrew word for "judge" also meant "deliverer" (Acts 7:35), as in the book of Judges, and was often a synonym for "ruler" in the Old Testament as well as in ancient Canaanite texts.

The other New Testament passage, Hebrews 11:24-27, reminds us that Moses was willing to share his people's mistreatment and suffering, that disgrace was acceptable to Moses because he knew that Christ was in some sense present with him, and that although "Moses was afraid" (v. 14), his fear of the king's anger was only impulsive and temporary because he knew he was being protected by the God who is invisible (Heb. 11:27).

The land of "Midian" (v. 15), to which Moses fled, was named after one of Abraham's younger sons (Gen. 25:2) and was located in southeastern Sinai and west central Arabia, flanking the Gulf of Aqaba on both sides. It was mostly a desert land and contrasted starkly with his former home in fertile Goshen. As he began his forty-year stay there (Acts 7:29-30), he performed an act of chivalry that gained him a wife named "Zipporah" (v. 21), which means "Lady Bird," a father-in-law who was a "priest of Midian" (v. 16) and whose name was "Reuel" (v. 18), meaning "Friend of God," and a son named "Gershom" (v. 22), which perhaps means "An Alien There" and refers to Moses' realization that he, somewhat homesick and lonely, was "an alien in a foreign land."

The "king of Egypt" in verse 23 is probably still Thutmose III, who enjoyed a long reign (about 1490-1436 B.C.). When the pharaoh died, the time became ripe for the Lord to act on behalf of His suffering people. He had promised their forefathers that the Israelites would become a great nation (Gen. 12:2), and He had formalized that promise by making a "covenant" (v. 24) with Abraham (Gen. 15:18; 17:7), a covenant He confirmed with Isaac (Gen. 17:19) and with Jacob (Gen. 35:11-12). God was now about to demonstrate that He never forgets His covenant promises.

2. *Moses' call* (3:1—4:17). The call of God to us is always personal and individual, and our response to Him must be similarly personal and individual. So it was with Moses.

God's Initiative (3:1-10). Moses was still working for his father-in-law (v. 1), here called "Jethro" (perhaps a title meaning "His Excellency"), near "Horeb, the mountain of God." Horeb (which means "Desolation") may be another name for Mount Sinai, although tradition equates it with a different mountain in the same area in the southeast Sinai peninsula, Ras es-Safsaf ("Willow Peak"), 6500 feet high, whereas Mount Sinai is usually claimed to be Jebel Musa ("Mountain of Moses"), 7400 feet high. Both identifications, however, are uncertain. At Horeb the "angel of the LORD" (v. 2) appeared to Moses. Since the angel of the Lord is often also referred to as "God" or "the LORD" in Scripture (see, for example, v. 4), many interpreters believe that the angel was Jesus in a preincarnation form. Although that is possible, such an interpretation dilutes the uniqueness of Jesus' incarnation and undercuts the teaching of Hebrews 1:3-14, where God's Son is said to be superior to all the angels. Because the Hebrew word for "angel" also means "messenger," it seems best to understand the angel of the Lord as a special divine messenger from the court of heaven and therefore representing the Lord, bearing His credentials and speaking on His behalf.

The locale of the revelation was "flames of fire" (v. 2), as it often was elsewhere in the Bible (Exod. 13:21; 19:18; 1 Kings 18:24, 38; see also Acts 2:3-4). God "called" Moses, as He did every true prophet (Gen. 12:1; 1 Sam. 3:4; Isa. 6:8; Jer. 1:4-5; Ezek. 2:1; Hos. 1:2; Amos 7:15; Jonah 1:1-2). The Lord repeated Moses' name for emphasis, and God's servant responded, "Here I am" (v. 4). So it was also with Abraham

(Gen. 22:11), with Jacob (Gen. 46:2), and with Samuel (1 Sam. 3:4, 10). In Moses' case, he was told to take off his sandals (a practice still followed by Muslims before entering a mosque) since the ground was "holy" (v. 5), not by nature but by divine appointment, because holiness involves removal from the commonplace to be set apart for serving God.

When the Lord identified Himself, Moses "was afraid to look at God" (v. 6) because to see God's face was believed to put the viewer in mortal danger (Gen. 16:13; 32:30; Judg. 13:22), as the Lord Himself affirmed to Moses (Exod. 33:20, 23). God would soon bring His people to "a land flowing with milk and honey" (v. 8), the traditional description of the hill country of Canaan in its original pastoral state. There Israel would meet the six enemy nations named here (see also Judg. 3:5). The number is elsewhere expanded to ten (Gen. 15:19-21) or even twelve (Gen. 10:15-18), but the classic list includes seven, the number of completion (Deut. 7:1). God told Moses to "go" (v. 10; see also Isa. 6:9; Jer. 2:2; Jonah 1:2; 3:2; Matt. 28:19) and proclaim the Lord's demands to the new pharaoh, probably Amunhotep II. (The accession date usually assigned to him [1438 B.C.] and the early date for the Exodus [1445 B.C.] do not precisely coincide because both dates are only approximate.)

Moses' Objections (3:11—4:17). The reluctant elderly (Exod. 7:7) shepherd now responded to God's call by voicing a series of five objections, the first of which concerned his own insignificance: "Who am I?" (v. 11). The Lord's all-sufficient answer was, "I will be with you" (v. 12; see Gen. 26:3, 24; 28:15; 31:3; Jer. 1:8, 19; Matt. 28:20; Acts 18:10). The Hebrew word translated "I will be" in verse 12 is the same as the one translated "I am" in verse 14. To His promise God added a "sign" (v. 12), a visible guarantee that what He had promised He would surely fulfill.

Moses' second objection expressed his uncertainty concerning how he should respond if his fellow Israelites should ask him what God's name was. Their question would relate not so much to God's title as it would to His nature, character, and qualities, since a name in biblical days was much more than simply a label. Again, God's all-sufficient answer was, "I am who I am," "I will be who I will be," the Hebrew way of saying, "I am he who is"—that is, "I am really and truly present, ready to help and to act,"[2] "I am the God who relates himself to you,[3] the God who is with you" (see again v. 12).

When used by God in the Bible, "I am" never refers merely to His existence or inscrutability or changelessness or sovereignty. Although it is of course true that anyone who comes to God "must believe that he exists" (Heb. 11:6*a*), it is also true that anyone who comes to God must believe "that he rewards those who earnestly seek him" (Heb. 11:6*b*). As James 2:19 puts the matter, "You believe that there is one God. Good! Even the demons believe that—and shudder." God's "I am" is always an expression of relationship to His people (see especially Exod. 34:5-7). The same Hebrew word is used in Exodus 4:12, 15, where the text says, literally, "I will be with your mouth."

In Exodus 3 God next gives two related names for Himself: *Ehyeh,* "I AM" (v. 14), and *Yahweh,* "THE LORD" (v. 15). The first is the same Hebrew word that is found in Exodus 3:12; 4:12, 15, and is used by God when He refers to Himself. The second is the third-person verbal form of the same word, means literally "HE IS," and is to be used by God's people when they refer to Him.[4] The two names are therefore different forms of the same Hebrew verb and constitute the most

---

2. Frederic William Bush, " 'I Am Who I Am': Moses and the Name of God," *Theology, News and Notes,* December 1976, p. 12.

3. Ronald Youngblood, "A New Occurrence of the Divine Name 'I AM,' " *Journal of the Evangelical Theological Society* 15 (Summer 1972): 144-52.

4. "The LORD" as a translation for *Yahweh* entered English versions from the Greek translation of the Old Testament known as the Septuagint. The incorrect vocalization of *Yahweh* as *Yehowah* (*Jehovah*) came about when Hebrew scribes during the Middle Ages combined the vowels of *Adonay* (another Hebrew word for "Lord") with the consonants of *Yahweh* since the latter was considered too sacred to pronounce.

intimate and personal name of God in Scripture. We can readily understand, then, why the Jews of Jesus' day thought our Lord was blaspheming when He said to them, "Before Abraham was born, I am" (John 8:58). Their reaction was to reach for rocks in order to stone Him. Our response should always be to fall at His feet in order to worship Him.

Moses was to repeat God's words to Israel's "elders" (v. 16). The Hebrew term means literally "bearded ones," perhaps reflecting the age, wisdom, experience, and community respect necessary for a man expected to function as the head of a family, clan, or tribe in matters of judicial arbitration (Deut. 22:13-19) as well as military leadership (Josh. 8:10) and counsel (1 Sam. 4:3). The "wonders" (v. 20) that God intended to perform among the Egyptians were the ten plagues that He would send against them (Exod. 7:14–12:30). By contrast, the Israelites would not leave Egypt "empty-handed" (v. 21) but would "plunder the Egyptians" (v. 22; see also 11:2-3; 12:35-36), as God had promised Abraham they would (Gen. 15:14; see also Ps. 105:37).

The third objection voiced by Moses was his fear that the Israelites might not believe him or listen to him (4:1). That time the Lord graciously gave Moses the ability to perform three miraculous signs that, either individually or in combination, would compel belief—even though God had earlier assured Moses that at least the elders would listen to him (Exod. 3:18).

The first sign would be the power to turn a staff (probably Moses' shepherd's crook) into a snake and then to reverse the process (vv. 2-5). A different Hebrew word for "snake" is used in Exodus 7:9-10 and is later translated "monster" as a nickname for Egypt and her king (Ezek. 29:3; see also Ps. 74:13). Egypt's pharaohs often wore metal cobras on the front of their crowns as a symbol of sovereignty.

The second sign would be Moses' ability to turn his hand "leprous" (v. 6) and then to reverse the process ("leprosy" in the Bible refers to a wide range of skin ailments, some of which were virtually incurable).

The third sign would be the power to turn some Nile water into blood—an ominous foregleam of the first of the ten plagues (Exod. 7:14-24). The term "miraculous sign" (v. 8), applicable to all three signs, is a specific Hebrew word referring to a supernatural phenomenon or event intended to encourage faith, demonstrate authority, provide assurance (Josh. 2:12-13), bear witness (Isa. 19:19-20), or give warning (Num. 17:10).

Fourth, Moses told God that he felt inadequate for the task: "I am slow of speech and tongue" (v. 10). Moses probably did not have a speech impediment, since Stephen later declared that Moses was "powerful in speech" (Acts 7:22). He objected instead that he was not eloquent or articulate enough to impress the pharaoh (see also Exod. 6:12). Similarly, some said of Paul, "In person he is unimpressive and his speaking amounts to nothing" (2 Cor. 10:10). But God, always patient, responded graciously to Moses by gently reminding him that it is the Lord Himself who gives a man his mouth and enables him to speak. He said to Moses, "I will be [*Ehyeh*—the divine name] with your mouth" (v. 12).

In Moses' fourth and fifth objections he addressed God by using the less personal form of the word translated "Lord" (vv. 10, 13; Hebrew *Adonay*). He seems to have been deliberately avoiding the powerful implications of the names *Ehyeh* and *Yahweh,* which God continually uses of Himself throughout this entire section (Exod. 3:12, 14-16, 18; 4:5, 11-12, 15). And Moses' fifth and final objection summed up all the others: "Send someone else" (v. 13). His earlier reasons were merely excuses, because he did not want God to send him in the first place. The Lord, though "slow to anger" (Exod. 34:6), now became angry with Moses—not because He had lost His temper but because Moses needed to be impressed with the seriousness of God's call and to learn that God is not to be trifled with. The Lord's final response, then, was just as gracious and loving as the previous four: He would provide Moses with a helper and companion, Moses' own brother, Aaron, three years his senior (Exod. 7:7). Just as a prophet is God's mouthpiece (Deut. 18:17-18; see also Exod. 7:1-2), so also Aaron would be Moses' mouthpiece (vv. 15-16). God concluded His response by reassuring Moses of his newly-granted power to "perform miraculous signs" (v. 17).

3. *Moses' return to Egypt* (4:18-31). Shorn of every valid excuse he might have had, Moses requested his father-in-law's permission to return to his people in Egypt (v. 18). All the men who had wanted to kill Moses, including Thutmose III (Exod. 2:23), were now dead (v. 19; for a striking later parallel, see Matt. 2:20). So Moses began his journey accompanied by Zipporah and his "sons" (plural, v. 20), Gershom (Exod. 2:22) and Eliezer (who, though not mentioned by name until Exod. 18:4, had obviously already been born). The name "Eliezer" means "My God Is My Help," a further reminder to Moses of where his strength was to be found. The family's pack animal was a donkey (v. 20), the main beast of burden in many parts of the Middle East from the Bronze Age to the present time. (The hardening of the pharaoh's heart, first mentioned in Exodus 4:21, will be discussed in the commentary at 7:3.)

In a striking phrase, God refers to Israel as His "firstborn son" (v. 22), not first of course in chronological order but in rank and preeminence with all the rights and responsibilities of the firstborn. Jacob (later renamed "Israel") was born after Esau (Gen. 25:25-26) and yet by implication is also called "firstborn" in Jeremiah 31:9. Since the pharaoh would refuse to emancipate God's "firstborn son," the Lord would kill the pharaoh's "firstborn son" (v. 23). The word "son" is here used collectively of the Israelites as a whole (see also Hos. 11:1), and therefore a collective understanding of the pharaoh's "son" is probably intended also—especially since the plague on the firstborn affected the entire land of Egypt (Exod. 11:5; 12:29).

We now learn that Moses' own life came to be in danger as well (v. 24). The Lord was "about to kill him," presumably because Moses had failed to circumcise his own son (whether Gershom or Eliezer we cannot tell) in clear disobedience to God's specific command and in violation of the Abrahamic covenant (Gen. 17:9-14, 23-27). Before Moses could return to Egypt to rescue the covenant people as their acknowledged leader, he himself must obey the covenant in every detail. Zipporah apparently understood that as well, because she sensed the reason for God's displeasure with her husband and therefore proceeded quickly to "cut off her son's foreskin" (v. 25). She used a "flint knife," evidently because the practice of circumcision went all the way back to the Stone Age (see also Josh. 5:2-3) and because stone implements continued to be used for ceremonial purposes long after bronze was introduced into human culture. Although after his son's circumcision Moses' life was spared, Zipporah seemed to have found the ceremony itself personally repulsive, since she called her husband "a bridegroom of blood" (v. 25).

Continuing on his journey, Moses met Aaron at the "mountain of God" (v. 27), doubtless near the place where he himself had first met God in a remarkable way (Exod. 3:1-2) and where he would soon meet Him again (Exod. 19:2-3), as God had promised (Exod. 3:12). Moses brought Aaron up to date concerning his recent experiences with the Lord, and then the two men, after arriving in Goshen, convened "all the elders of the Israelites" (v. 29). Aaron, beginning his duties as Moses' spokesman, told the elders everything the Lord had said to his brother. Exodus 4 closes with the people of Israel bowing down in an attitude of worship, faith, and expectancy.

4

CONFRONTATION

C. GOD CONFRONTS PHARAOH (5:1—12:30)

Having found favor with his brother, Aaron, with the elders of Israel, and with the people themselves (Exod. 4:27-31), Moses was now ready to serve as the Lord's ambassador to Pharaoh's court. He would not receive the same cordial response there that he did from his fellow Israelites, however. Moses would soon learn that the struggle between God and the pharaoh was just beginning.

1. *Pharaoh hardens his heart* (5:1—7:13). The Egyptian ruler—an absolute monarch, proud and unyielding, believing himself to be a god—refused to listen to the Lord and His servant Moses. As his resistance stiffened, the way was prepared for the horror of the ten plagues.

Moses Meets Pharaoh (5:1-21). The divine command that Moses and Aaron were to deliver to the pharaoh on their first meeting with him was simple and direct: "Let my people go." It was given a total of seven times (Exod. 5:1; 7:16; 8:1, 20; 9:1, 13; 10:3) and has continued to punctuate history's cries for freedom like a stirring refrain down to the present. In Exodus its primary intention is spiritual: God wanted His people set free "so that they may hold a festival to me in the desert" (v. 1)—that is, "so that they may worship me" (Exod. 7:16; 8:1, 20; 9:1, 13; 10:3). In every case, then, freedom of worship—the most basic of all freedoms—is in view.

The pharaoh, of course, paid no attention to the demands

of Moses and Aaron. He gave two reasons for refusing their request: He did not acknowledge the sovereignty of the God of the Hebrews over Egypt (v. 2), and he did not want to lose his enormous pool of cheap labor (vv. 4-5). He suspected that Moses was using "a three-day journey into the desert" (v. 3) as a ploy to gain total freedom for the Israelites. Moses' rationale for wanting to sacrifice to the Lord in an area far away from the main Egyptian population was that Israelite sacrifices "would be detestable to the Egyptians" (Exod. 8:26; see also Gen. 43:32).

As it turned out, the demand of Moses and Aaron backfired. The pharaoh decided to use it as an excuse for making the work of the Israelites harder than before. He did that not by requiring them to make bricks without the use of straw (a common misunderstanding of the account in Exodus 5) but by forcing them to "go and gather their own straw" (v. 7). Mud bricks, especially of the sun-dried variety, do not hold up well without using something like straw as binder. The "slave drivers" (v. 6) who were to carry out the pharaoh's order were probably the same as the Egyptian "slave masters" of Exodus 1:11, whereas the "foremen" were Israelite supervisors who had been appointed by the slave drivers and who were responsible for making sure that the Israelite laborers met a specified daily quota of bricks (v. 14). Israel's hopes for an early release from their bondage were labeled as "lies" by the pharaoh (v. 9). The "stubble" (v. 12) that they gathered was poorer and coarser than straw, making their work even more difficult. But in spite of everything they were not permitted to reduce their daily production quota (vv. 8, 11, 13-14, 18-19). The Israelite foremen complained that Moses and Aaron had made them "a stench" (v. 21) to the pharaoh and his officials (for a similar warning see Gen. 34:30).

The Lord Encourages Moses (5:22—7:9). God had told Moses earlier that the pharaoh would not accede to the divine demands until drastic measures were taken (Exod. 3:18-20), but Moses had apparently forgotten. Impatiently he voiced some of his earlier complaints (5:22-23).

After reminding Moses of the earlier promises (6:1; see 3:19-20), the Lord gave him a new and highly significant revelation of Himself and His name (6:2-8). Four times He said to Moses, "I am the LORD": to introduce Himself and His message (v. 2), to reaffirm His promise to redeem (v. 6) based on the evidence of verses 2-5, to stress His intention to adopt Israel as His covenant people (v. 7), and to conclude His message after reasserting His promise to give Israel the land of Canaan (v. 8). The Israelites would learn to know God in a new way as "the LORD." The pharaoh also, who at the outset claimed to know nothing about the Lord (5:2), would learn about Him (6:29)—and very soon at that (7:3-5).

During the patriarchal period the characteristic name of God was "God Almighty" (6:3; see, for example, Gen. 17:1), the usual English translation of the Hebrew *El Shaddai,* which probably literally means "God, the Mountain One." That phrase could refer to the mountains as God's symbolic home (see Ps. 121:1), but it more likely stresses His invincible power and might. God as *El Shaddai* controls nature and history as He acts on behalf of His people from the most ancient times. *Shaddai* occurs thirty-one times in the book of Job (who was a patriarch) alone and seventeen times in the rest of the Old Testament (six of those occurrences are in Genesis).

But during the Mosaic period the characteristic name of God was to be "the LORD," the meaning of which was first revealed to Moses himself (Exod. 3:13-15). Exodus 6:3 is not saying that the patriarchs were totally ignorant of the name *Yahweh.* Verses such as Exodus 3:15-16; 4:5 go out of their way to equate the God of the patriarchs with "the LORD." Even non-Hebrews, such as the king of Sodom and—by implication—Melchizedek (Gen. 14:19, 22), were familiar with the name. Recently interpreted evidence from Amorite texts (from Mari on the Euphrates, for example) dating to the patriarchal period makes it likely that the equivalent of the name *Yahweh* was known among the Amorites, whereas the shortened form of *Yahweh* (*Yah*) appears to occur even earlier on tablets from Ebla in northern Syria in names such as *Mi-ka-ya* (compare biblical "Micaiah"), which means "Who Is Like Yah?" We read that earlier still, when the human race was in its infancy, "at that time men began to call on the name of the LORD" (Gen. 4:26).

It would seem, therefore, that the name *Yahweh* is very ancient indeed. But if that is so, what are we to make of God's statement to Moses, "By my name the LORD I did not make myself known to" Abraham, Isaac, and Jacob (Exod. 6:3)? That verse is especially puzzling when we note that *"Yahweh"* occurs dozens of times in the patriarchal narratives of Genesis 12-50 and is, in fact, the first name by which God is identified in them (Gen. 12:1).

The key to answering that question lies in the basic meaning of the verb "to know" in Scripture. Knowledge is of two kinds: casual (knowledge by acquaintance) and intimate (knowledge by experience). The patriarchs (and doubtless others before them) had a more or less casual knowledge of the name *Yahweh*, but not until the time of Moses would the descendants of the patriarchs come to know that name in all of its rich meaning and application. Exodus 6:2-8 makes clear that the name *Yahweh* emphasizes the activity of God as the One who would redeem His people, and that fact could only be fully understood by the Israelites who were about to experience the Exodus. From the very moment of Israel's emancipation from Egyptian slavery, the name *Yahweh* would signify "Redeemer" to God's people.[1] When therefore God said, "By my name the LORD I did not make myself known to" the patriarchs, He was simply saying that He did not

---

1. A similar experiential sense of the verb "to know" is evident also in its use throughout the story of the plagues (Exod. 7:17; 8:10, 22; 9:14, 29; 10:2; 11:7) and in connection with the Exodus itself (14:4, 18; 16:6, 8, 12; 18:11).

reveal to them the full significance of that name.

Through Moses the Lord told His people what He was about to do for them, and His "I will" is repeated seven times throughout this passage, each time linked to a redemptive act: "I will bring you out . . . I will free you . . . [I] will redeem you . . . I will take you as my own people . . . I will be your God . . . I will bring you to the land . . . I will give it to you" (vv. 6-8). The Exodus therefore became the supreme example of God's activity as Redeemer in the Old Testament. God's irresistible plan and irreversible intention was to bring His people out (of slavery in Egypt) in order to bring them in (to freedom in Canaan). And so we are reminded that redemption is not only release from slavery and suffering but also deliverance to freedom and joy. In addition, God's "mighty acts of judgment" (v. 6; see also Exod. 7:4) involved not only redemption for Israel but also judgment against Egypt.

When the Lord said, "I will take you as my own people, and I will be your God" (v. 7), He was using words that anticipated the establishment of the covenant with Israel at Mount Sinai (Exod. 19:5-6; see also Jer. 30:22; 31:1, 33; 32:38; Ezek. 36:28; 37:23; Hos. 2:23). Centuries earlier God had sworn "with uplifted hand" (v. 8) that He would give Canaan to Abraham's descendants (Gen. 22:15-17). Solemnly raising the right hand was the standard oath-taking practice in ancient times (Gen. 14:22; Deut. 32:40; Rev. 10:5-6) and remains so today. Despite everything, however, the people of Israel were discouraged and unimpressed when Moses reported to them what God had promised (v. 9).

The genealogy that follows in Exodus 6:14-25 is beautifully framed by the repetition in 6:26-30 of the same information (and often the same phraseology) that appears in 6:10-13. Especially interesting is Moses' complaint that he was "uncircumcised of lips" (6:12, repeated in 6:30). This is the first example in the Bible of a reference to circumcision in other than the physical sense. The basic purpose of physical circumcision seems to have been the removal of actual or potential uncleanness, and therefore the word "circumcision" and related terms are sometimes used in the figurative sense of the removal of ethical or spiritual uncleanness. For example, we read of circumcised "hearts" (Deut. 10:16) and of uncircumcised "ears" (Jer. 6:10). Similarly, Paul defines "we who are the circumcision" as "we who worship by the Spirit of God, who glory in Christ Jesus, and who put no confidence in the flesh" (Phil. 3:3). In Moses' case (vv. 12, 30) he appears to have been simply repeating in different words his old objection that he lacked the eloquence he needed to talk to the pharaoh (see 4:10).

Verses 26-27 (see also v. 13) tell us that the purpose of the genealogy recorded in verses 14-25 is to give us pertinent details concerning the family background of the specific Moses and the specific Aaron about whom the book of Exodus speaks. The genealogy therefore treats only the first three of Jacob's twelve sons (Reuben, Simeon, and Levi) since Moses and Aaron are from the third tribe.

Several of the names listed are of Egyptian origin, including "Merari" (v. 16), "Putiel," and "Phinehas" (v. 25), not to mention that of Moses himself, who was given his name by a pharaoh's daughter (2:10). The name of Moses' mother, "Jochebed" (v. 20), is clearly Semitic, however. The name means "The LORD Is Glory" and demonstrates once again (see the commentary on v. 3) that the name *Yahweh* (here abbreviated as *Jo-*) was at least casually known before Moses was born. (Aaron is listed before Moses in verse 20 because he is the older of the two—see 7:7—and such genealogies were official documents used for legal purposes.) Levi's life span is given because it exceeded one hundred years (6:16; see also vv. 18, 20). The genealogy begins with a title (v. 14*a*) and ends with a brief summary (v. 25*b*).

As chapter 7 opens, the Lord responds to Moses' objection in 6:30 in much the same way as He had to Moses' similar objection in 4:10, 13. Just as God has His prophets who proclaim His word to His people (Deut. 18:18), so Moses would have Aaron as his "prophet" (v. 1) to speak to the pharaoh on his behalf (v. 2). Just as Moses was God's mouthpiece, so Aaron would be Moses' mouthpiece (4:14-16). But the pharaoh would not respond favorably to Moses' words because, says the Lord, "I will harden Pharaoh's heart" (v. 3).

The hardening of the pharaoh's heart has been a subject of theological discussion and debate for centuries. The book of Exodus appears to attribute the hardening process nine times to God (4:21; 7:3; 9:12; 10:1, 20, 27; 11:10; 14:4, 8) and an equal number of times to the pharaoh himself (7:13, 14, 22; 8:15, 19, 32; 9:7, 34, 35). The problem is that God seems to have begun the process (4:21; 7:3) before the pharaoh joined in (7:13), and therefore some interpreters believe that this series of events is an example of divine negative predestination: The pharaoh is simply a pawn with no will of his own, a puppet forced by God to harden his heart against his own desires—since God is sovereign and does whatever He pleases (Ps. 135:6).

But God, though sovereign, does not violate a person's free will. Exodus tells us that God hardened the pharaoh's heart, but it also tells us that the pharaoh hardened his own heart and did so willfully and repeatedly. Let us therefore examine the eighteen references more closely.

The first two (4:21; 7:3) state that God "will harden" the pharaoh's heart at some future time (without specifying when that will be). The next ten references (the only exception is 9:12) indicate that the pharaoh hardened his own heart. The final six references tell us that God "hardened" (past tense, the only exception being 14:4) the pharaoh's heart. The picture that emerges, then, is that God, on the basis of His foreknowledge, predicted (4:21; 7:3) and announced that He would harden the pharaoh's heart, but only after the pharaoh had hardened his own heart (the next ten references). God then confirmed that hardening process (the last six references), beginning His own involvement in it (9:12) after the pharaoh's willful hardening had passed the point of no return. Although mankind's sin is God's sorrow, the time comes when God gives hopelessly wicked people over to "sexual impurity" (Rom. 1:24), to "shameful lusts" (1:26), to "a depraved mind" (1:28)—the ultimate outcome of which is "death" (1:32) and "God's judgment" (2:2). In the pharaoh's case God foreknew that Egypt's king would harden his heart, and the pharaoh proceeded to do so—knowingly, willfully, and sinfully (Exod. 9:34). God then confirmed the pharaoh's action through His own judicial hardening of the pharaoh's heart.

Paul reasoned that God hardened the pharaoh's heart in a free and sovereign manner but not in a capricious or arbitrary manner (Rom. 9:14-18). He always acts justly (9:14) and in sovereign freedom (9:18). He displays "great patience" toward "the objects of his wrath" (9:22). He was about to give the pharaoh numerous opportunities to free the people of Israel but He knew in advance that the pharaoh would choose to do otherwise. The pharaoh would therefore be compelled to bear full responsibility for that willful and sinful choice (Exod. 10:7).

The pharaoh hardened his heart in spite of the "miraculous signs and wonders" (7:3) that God was about to "multiply" in Egypt. The word "miracle" may be defined as an extraordinary event in physical space and historical time caused by the supernatural power of God. Such miracles were "multiplied" during four main periods of biblical history: the time of the early divided monarchy (the days of Elijah and Elisha, when those who believed in the one true God and those who worshiped Canaanite deities such as Baal and Asherah were struggling for spiritual supremacy in Israel); the time of the exile (when Daniel and his godly companions refused to worship the deities of Babylon and Persia); the time of Jesus and the apostles (when the battle was between the Son of God and His followers on the one hand and Satan and his minions on the other); and, of course, the time of the Exodus (when the pharaoh needed to be driven to his knees with the realization that the God of the Hebrews was superior in every way to all the deities of Egypt, including the pharaoh himself). In the case of the Exodus, many miracles come immediately to mind: the hand that became leprous, the staff that turned into a snake, the ten plagues, the pillar of cloud and the pillar of fire, the division of the waters of the Sea of Reeds, and more.

When we observe that Moses and Aaron, the two men through whom God had chosen to mediate His messages and miracles to the pharaoh, were eighty and eighty-three years old respectively (Exod. 7:7), the account of the struggle becomes all the more remarkable. Humanly speaking, their ages put them at a decided disadvantage—but with God on their side, not even a powerful pharaoh could succeed (Rom. 8:31).

Moses Meets Pharaoh Again (7:10-13). The basic pattern established in this paragraph in Exodus will be repeated in one form or other in connection with each of the ten plagues. Moses and/or Aaron will perform a miracle to demonstrate that God is superior to the pharaoh and his gods; the pharaoh's magicians will try to duplicate the miracle "by their secret arts," or the plague caused by the miracle will subside, in either case bringing relief to the Egyptians; the pharaoh will harden his heart further and continue to refuse to free the Israelites; and Moses and/or Aaron will then perform another miracle, bringing on the next plague.

Aaron began the sequence by throwing down his staff in front of the pharaoh. It became a snake (v. 10), just as it had when Moses had thrown it down earlier (4:3). In this case, however, the Egyptian magicians were able to do "the same things" by means of their secret arts (v. 11). Egyptian magicians were mentioned centuries earlier in the days of Joseph (Gen. 41:8, 24), and Babylonian magicians were to be found centuries later in the days of Daniel (Dan. 2:10, 27; 4:7; 5:11). Such men were learned members of the royal court, perhaps priests who claimed to possess occult knowledge. Two of the magicians who "opposed Moses" were named "Jannes and Jambres" (2 Tim. 3:8). Their ability to duplicate Aaron's miracle may have been by throwing down stiffened snakes that they had earlier paralyzed by putting pressure on certain nerves in their necks. Perhaps they used sleight of hand, or possibly demonic power was involved. In any event, Aaron's staff demonstrated the superior power of Israel's God by swallowing up the magicians' staffs (v. 12).

But the pharaoh—unimpressed—hardened his heart, and so the Lord increased the pressure on him by announcing the first of the ten plagues.

5

PLAGUES

EXODUS 7:14—11:10; 12:29-30

2. *The ten plagues* (7:14—12:30). Although there were ten plagues in all, the tenth was climactic and is therefore described at greater length (11:1—12:30). The narrative of the tenth plague is interwoven with the account of the institution of the Passover (12:1-28), the discussion of which will be left to the next chapter.

The story of the plagues is summarized in Psalm 78:44-51, where six of them are mentioned specifically (though not in chronological order): the blood, the flies, the frogs, the locusts, the hail, the death of the firstborn. The story is summarized also in Psalm 105:28-36, where this time eight plagues are mentioned (again, not in chronological order): the darkness, the blood, the frogs, the flies, the gnats, the hail, the locusts, the death of the firstborn. In both psalms the plague on the firstborn is mentioned last to stress its climactic importance. In Psalms 135:8 and 136:10 it is the only plague referred to at all, apparently because its story in Exodus made a much greater impression on later generations than the accounts of the other plagues did. The tenth plague can therefore stand for all the plagues because it was the most astounding and destructive of them all (see also Heb. 11:28).

Psalms 78, 105, 135, and 136 are hymns of praise to the Lord for His miraculous deeds that preserved and strengthened His people. The plagues, then, were remembered in Israel's later history and were joyfully celebrated as unusual examples of God's provision for His people's needs. (Elsewhere in the Bible, in Revelation 8-9 and 15-16, a series of cosmic plagues resembling some of the Exodus plagues is announced by seven trumpets and poured out on the earth from the seven bowls of God's wrath in the last days.)

The ten plagues had several purposes as described in Exodus itself. The Lord sent the plagues to judge Egypt and her gods (Exod. 7:4; 10:2; 12:12; 18:11), and we will note that many of the individual plagues seem to have been directed against a specific Egyptian deity. Needless to say, the plagues were also used by God to compel the pharaoh to free the Israelites (7:4; 18:10). Third, they were sent to prove once and for all that God Himself is the only sovereign Lord of nature and history (7:5; 9:14-15; 10:2; 18:11). Fourth, the plagues struck the land of Goshen selectively, making a distinction between Egypt and Israel and demonstrating that the Israelites were God's chosen people, who came under His protective care (8:22-23; 11:7; 12:27). Finally, the plagues displayed the Lord's almighty power and proclaimed His holy name (9:16).

A certain progression may be observed as the Exodus plague narrative unfolds. The pharaoh's magicians were able to duplicate the first two plagues but were stopped by the third (8:18). The Lord mediated the first three plagues through Moses and Aaron but then began to play a more active role with the fourth plague. By the time of the tenth plague Moses simply made the announcement to the pharaoh, Aaron receded entirely into the background (11:10 merely summarizes the preceding nine plagues), and God was the sole actor. After each of the first five plagues the pharaoh hardened his own heart, but after each of the last five plagues (the seventh is the only exception) God confirmed that hardening. There was a general increase in the intensity and severity of each successive plague as time went on.

Although the pharaoh's heart was hardened after each of the plagues was past, his skills as a negotiator are evident in his successive responses to Moses' request that the Israelites be allowed to take a three-day journey into the desert to offer sacrifices to the Lord. The first plague was relatively mild, and the pharaoh's answer was an implicit but nevertheless categorical "No." During the second plague he agreed to release the Israelites, but only if the frogs were taken away (8:8). During the fourth plague he again agreed, but only if the people did not "go very far" (8:28). The seventh plague caused the pharaoh to admit his sin and to agree once again to let the people go—but only if the hailstorm ceased (9:27-28). During the eighth plague he agreed to free only the men (10:11), and during the ninth plague he expressed his willingness to release the women and children also—but only if the flocks and herds were left behind (10:24). Only the devastation of the tenth plague could force the pharaoh to free all the people, their flocks and herds, and only the tenth plague could wring from him the plaintive request to Moses: "And also bless me" (12:32).

The first nine plagues can be grouped into three sets of three apiece (the writer himself probably intended such a division). The first plague in each set—numbers one, four, and seven—was introduced with a warning by Moses to the pharaoh in the morning as the pharaoh went out to the Nile (7:15; 8:20; 9:13). By contrast, the last plague in each set—numbers three, six and nine—was unannounced to the pharaoh. The first three plagues were related to the Nile and its associated pools and streams, the next three were concerned with flies and the diseases they carry, and the final three described phenomena that produced increasing degrees of darkness.

Recent studies of the first nine plagues indicate that they may have been a series of calamities similar to the kinds that have struck Egypt from the remotest times. If so, God supernaturally heightened them and brought them on the scene at His own bidding and timing (probably all of them taking place in less than a year). They were not merely natural disasters, of course, because to claim so would be to remove them from the realm of the miraculous and downgrade them to sheer coincidence.

Although in nearly every case each plague could have

resulted from the effects of the preceding plague or plagues on the basis of what we know about Egyptian geography, climate, and the like,[1] the details of the account make it clear that the God of miracles, who gave Moses and Aaron the power to bend natural phenomena to accomplish His will, was working out His purposes for His people in and through the sequence of events from the very beginning. Each plague, then, was a true "miracle," which we defined earlier as "an extraordinary event in physical space and historical time caused by the supernatural power of God." More specifically, the first nine plagues may be described as miracles of heightening and timing. Assuming the validity of this general approach, we may outline the sequence of the plagues as follows.

The first plague would have been caused by unusually severe flooding of the Nile in late summer and early fall, washing down large amounts of red sediment from the highlands of Ethiopia and so making the waters appear as red as blood (for a similar phenomenon see 2 Kings 3:22). Seven days later (Exod. 7:25) huge numbers of frogs would have abandoned the flooded and polluted Nile and swarmed over the land (second plague), probably because the unusually high concentration of bacteria-laden algae carried down by the waters had by that time proved fatal to most of the fish. By late autumn the high waters would also have flooded the fields adjacent to the river, providing excellent breeding grounds for enormous numbers of gnats (third plague).

"Swarms of flies" (8:21), probably *Stomoxys calcitrans,* would have multiplied rapidly as the receding Nile left breeding places in its wake (fourth plague). The flies would have also become carriers of the highly infectious and usually fatal *Bacillus anthracis* that had already killed the fish and frogs, and livestock (brought back into the fields as the flood-waters subsided) would have succumbed to the anthrax

---

1. See Greta Hort, "The Plagues of Egypt," *Zeitschrift für die alt-testamentliche Wissenschaft* 69 (1957): 84-103; 70 (1958): 48-59.

bacteria (fifth plague). A variety of the disease that infected the livestock would then have struck other animals as well as the Egyptian people themselves, causing boils to break out on their skin (sixth plague).

Since the flooding of the Nile would have come to an end late in the fall, the severe hailstorm (seventh plague) is in proper chronological position because it would have arrived in January or February, the time when the flax and barley crops would have been in full flower (and therefore destroyed by the hail), whereas the wheat and spelt would not yet have germinated (9:31-32). The prevailing east winds (10:13) of March or April would then have brought in hordes of migratory locusts (eighth plague) at the nymph stage, the most voracious time of their development. The three-day darkness (ninth plague) that followed would probably have been caused by the dreaded *khamsin,* the blinding sandstorm that blows in from the desert annually in the early spring.

Whether that or a similar reconstruction is correct we cannot know for certain, of course. In any case we insist that the disastrous plagues striking the Egyptians were subjected to supernatural heightening and split-second timing by the sovereign God of Israel, who brought them about at just the right time and with just the right intensity. We now want to examine the individual accounts of each of the nine plagues, as well as that of the tenth, in somewhat more detail.

a. The Plague of Blood (7:14-24). The word "blood" can be understood either as literal blood or metaphorically as "blood red" (that is, the color of blood). In either case the fish in the Nile would die (vv. 17-18). Since the Nile was worshiped as a god, polluting it would be an insult to Egyptian religious doctrine. The Hebrew text lying behind the last few words of verse 19 may be translated literally as "even in/on the wooden things and in/on the stone things." Egyptians believed in "images and idols of wood and stone" (Deut. 29:16-17), and therefore "blood" splashed on their objects of worship would have been considered a further rebuke to their religion. Only the Lord Himself, however, is worthy of wor-

ship (v. 17). To supply their needs for potable drinking water
the Egyptians were forced to dig "along the Nile" (v. 24),
because the polluted waters would become safe for drinking
only after being filtered through the sandy soil near the river
bank.

b. The Plague of Frogs (8:1-15). Since the frog or toad was
deified as the Egyptian goddess Heqt, who was believed to
assist women in childbirth, there may be a touch of irony in
the statement that large numbers of frogs would invade the
pharaoh's bedroom and even jump onto his bed (v. 3). Moses
challenged the pharaoh to choose the day for the removal of
the frogs from plaguing the Egyptians and ruining their
homes (v. 9), and God was therefore given another occasion
to demonstrate that He is sovereign over time (vv. 10-13).

c. The Plague of Gnats (8:16-19). Only God can make gnats
from "dust" (a word that may refer as well to the enormous
number of gnats produced—see, for example, Gen. 13:16).
When the magicians failed in their attempt to do the same,
they referred to Aaron's successful feat as the "finger of
God" (v. 19)—an excellent brief definition of a miracle (see
also 31:18). The "hand of the LORD" is used similarly in 9:3.
God uses His fingers when He creates (Ps. 8:3), reminding us
of *The Creation of Man,* Michelangelo's fresco on the ceiling
of the Sistine Chapel in Rome. On one occasion Jesus drove
out demons "by the finger of God" (Luke 11:20)—that is,
with God's help.

d. The Plague of Flies (8:20-32). For the first time we are
told that the Lord was making a distinction between the
Israelites and Eygptians by keeping the plague of flies away
from Goshen, where His people lived (vv. 22-23). In so doing,
God demonstrated His sovereignty over space as well as time
and preserved His own people while judging Egypt. (We are
doubtless justified in concluding that the first three plagues
did not harm the Israelites either.) The pharaoh, who prided
himself on being the main possessor of *maat* ("justice,"
"order") in Egypt, was chided by Moses not to act "deceit-

fully" (v. 29). When Moses prayed for the pharaoh, his prayer was answered (vv. 30-31; see also 1 Kings 18:42-45; Amos 7:1-6). "The prayer of a righteous man is powerful and effective" (James 5:16).

e. The Plague on Livestock (9:1-7). Once again Egypt's religion was rebuked and ridiculed, because it included the worship of various animals (such as the bull-gods, Apis and Mnevis; the cow-god, Hathor; and the ram-god, Khnum) as well as animal-headed deities. "All the livestock of the Egyptians died" (v. 6), except for the animals that were quarantined by removing them from areas infested with the anthrax bacteria (see similarly 9:19-21).

f. The Plague of Boils (9:8-12). Probably a variety of the bacteria that caused the previous plague, the boils may have been the result of skin anthrax, a black abscess that develops into a pustule. The "soot from a furnace" (v. 8), the immediate source of the boils, is perhaps doubly symbolic: The soot may symbolize the black coloration of the disease, and the furnace (probably a brick-firing kiln) may be a symbol of Israel's slavery (1:14; 5:7-19). The same word for "furnace" is used earlier as a simile for the destruction of Sodom and Gomorrah (Gen. 19:28). Moses refers to the boils again in Deuteronomy 28:27 (see also 7:15). They were very painful and seriously affected the knees, legs, and soles of the feet (Deut. 28:35)—which may explain why "the magicians could not stand before Moses" (v. 11).

g. The Plague of Hail (9:13-35). The pharaoh was allowed to remain alive, so that God might show the pharaoh His power and so that God's name might be proclaimed everywhere (v. 16). Paul quoted the verse almost verbatim as an outstanding illustration of God's sovereignty (Rom. 9:17). Some of the pharaoh's officials had begun to fear the word of the Lord and were taking measures to protect their slaves and livestock (v. 20). Although the damage done by the hailstorm was widespread and devastating (v. 25), a few trees remained for the locusts of the next plague to devour (10:5). The pharaoh acknowledged his sinfulness and his wicked deeds for the first time (v. 27), and Moses agreed to intercede for him by spreading out his hands to the Lord in prayer (vv. 29, 33). Statues of men praying with hands upraised have been unearthed at several ancient sites (see also 1 Kings 8:22, 38, 54; 2 Chron. 6:12-13, 29; Ezra 9:5; Pss. 44:20; 88:9; 143:6; Isa. 1:15). Grains of "spelt" (v. 32), a grass related to wheat, have been found in ancient Egyptian tombs.

h. The Plague of Locusts (10:1-20). Telling our children of God's miraculous deeds (v. 2) is an important means of keeping the memory of them alive for future generations (12:26-27; 13:8, 14-15; Deut. 4:9; Pss. 77:11-20; 78:43-53; 105:26-38; 106:7-12; 114:1-3; 135:8-9; 136:10-15). In ancient times a plague of locusts was a fearful disaster that could destroy an entire village's food supply in a few minutes (v. 5) and as such became a powerful symbol of divine judgment (Joel 1:1-7; 2:1-11; Amos 7:1-3). Even modern technology can do very little to stop the terrible devastation caused by locust hordes.[2]

The pharaoh's officials knew that "Egypt is ruined" (v. 7), and all because of the pharaoh's persistent and willful disobedience. He was willing to allow only Israel's men to leave Egypt for a few days (v. 11) because only they could participate fully in worship and because he wanted to retain the women and children as hostages to guarantee the men's return. The Lord brought in the locusts on "an east wind" (v. 13) and carried them away on a "west wind" (v. 19), compelling the forces of nature to obey His sovereign will (see also 14:21; Matt. 8:23-27).

i. The Plague of Darkness (10:21-29). The sun-god, Ra, was one of the most prominent Egyptian deities, and the sun itself has been one of the chief features of the climate of Egypt since time immemorial, warming and energizing her people. A plague of darkness, then, was yet another insult to

Egypt's religion and culture. It is ironic indeed that the pharaoh should choose to use such words as "sight," "appear," and "see" (v. 28) in the midst of "total darkness" (v. 22). Moses' response—"I will never appear before you again" (v. 29)—likewise contains a touch of poetic justice.

j. The Plague of the Firstborn (11:1-10; 12:29-30). Since all the plans and dreams of a family were bound up in the firstborn son, the tenth plague was the ultimate disaster. The laws of primogeniture decreed that the lion's share of the family estate would be inherited by the firstborn son when the father died (Deut. 21:17), so the death of the firstborn would cripple the family legally and emotionally. The tenth plague was therefore potentially more devastating than the first nine put together. It was also beautifully and selectively miraculous, because it destroyed only Egyptian firstborn males, whether human or animal—it did not touch Israelites, or any creatures other than firstborn, or female people or animals. The tenth plague was not simply a childhood disease that would reach epidemic proportions as it swept through Egypt, killing every young person in its path—it was much too selective for that. It would wipe out every Egyptian firstborn son, from the firstborn of the pharaoh to the firstborn of "the slave girl, who is at her hand mill" (v. 5), who had the lowliest of occupations (Isa. 47:2) and who was paralleled by "the prisoner . . . in the dungeon" (Exod. 12:29), who found himself in the lowliest of situations. None of the firstborn sons in Egypt, from highest to lowest, would escape the stroke of "the destroyer" (12:23).

By contrast, among the Israelites not even "a dog will bark at any man or animal" (11:7). Once again, and finally, the Lord "makes a distinction between Egypt and Israel" (v. 7).

6

PASSOVER

EXODUS 12:1-28; 12:43—13:16

II. FROM EGYPT TO SINAI: EMANCIPATION (12:31—18:27)

The second of the three main sections of Exodus forms the heart of the book. Although briefer than the other two sections, it describes Israel on the move and tells the remarkable story of how God made it possible for His people to flee Egypt, her pharaoh, his slave drivers and charioteers, and to begin their journey to Mount Sinai, eventually to arrive in the promised land of Canaan.

A. EXODUS AND PASSOVER (12:31—13:16)

Just as the narrative of the tenth plague is interwoven with the account of the institution of the Passover, so also the full and solemn description of the Passover and its associated ceremonies and regulations includes a brief passage outlining the first stage of Israel's escape from Egypt (12:31-42), the discussion of which will be postponed to the next chapter. Before proceeding to Exodus 12:43, however, we will turn back to 12:1-28, the story of the institution of the Passover, and consider it in some detail.

Passover: Institution (12:1-28). Since the exodus from Egypt would trigger the start of a whole new way of life for the people of Israel, God gave them a brand new calendar to symbolize their new beginning. From now on the "first month" of their year (v. 2) would be in the spring and is roughly equivalent to the thirty days from mid-March to mid-April. In Hebrew the month was called *Abib* (13:4; 23:15;

34:18; Deut. 16:1), which means "young head of grain" and reflects the fresh, life-giving nature of springtime. The name of the month was later changed to *Nisan* (Neh. 2:1; Esther 3:7), a Babylonian title that was still in use during the time of Jesus. The inauguration of Israel's religious calendar at the institution of the Passover did not eliminate her civil or agricultural calendar, which began in the fall at the end of the harvest season (Exod. 23:16). Both calendars—civil and religious—existed side by side until after the Babylonian exile (586 B.C.), but today Judaism uses only the calendar that begins in the fall.

The spring, however, was chosen by God for the time of the Exodus because it symbolized new life and burgeoning growth. It therefore became the time for Israel's national redemption from Egyptian slavery. The spring—the month of Nisan, in fact—was an equally suitable time for the resurrection of Jesus Christ, which likewise inaugurated a new religious calendar (this time a weekly calendar) by moving the Sabbath from the seventh day of the week to the first day (Acts 20:7; 1 Cor. 16:2), also called "the Lord's Day" (Rev. 1:10).

The technical term "community" (v. 3) is used of Israel assembled to worship the Lord. The main item in their Passover celebration was to be a lamb or young goat, chosen on the tenth day of the first month (v. 3) and slaughtered on the fourteenth (v. 6). It was to be a year-old male "without defect" (v. 5; see also Lev. 22:18-25), reminding us that Jesus was like "a lamb without blemish or defect" (1 Pet. 1:19). As Jesus' death was a sacrifice (1 Cor. 5:7), so also the Passover lamb was a sacrifice (Exod. 12:27; 34:25), not just part of a community meal or festival. It was to be slaughtered "at twilight" (v. 6), literally "between the two evening," meaning either in the late afternoon (between the decline of the sun and sunset) or between sunset and nightfall. The former fits better as prefiguring the time of the death of Jesus, which occurred at about three o'clock in the afternoon, the "ninth hour" (Matt. 27:45-46; Mark 15:33-34; Luke 23:44) of the day (which began at about six o'clock in the morning).

Some of the blood of the sacrificed animal was to be put "on the sides and tops of the doorframes" of the Israelite homes (v. 7). The Lord would then "pass over" (vv. 13, 23) the houses so marked on that same night, the night of the plague on the firstborn. The people's faith would result in their salvation (Heb. 11:28), since the blood of a sacrifice symbolizes the substitution of one life laid down for another (Lev. 17:11). Redemption, including the forgiveness of sin, takes place only when the blood of an innocent offering is shed (Heb. 9:22; 1 John 1:7). The "Passover lamb" (v. 21) typifies Jesus as "the Lamb of God, who takes away the sin of the world" (John 1:29, 35).

Although the main course in the Passover meal was the lamb (roasted according to the method used by wandering shepherds—v. 9), other items were to be included also. "Bitter herbs" (v. 8; Num. 9:11), such as endive, chicory, and other plants with a bitter taste, are native to Egypt, and eating them would recall the Israelites' bitter experience there (Exod. 1:14). "Bread made without yeast" (v. 8) reflects the haste required as the people prepared to leave (vv. 11, 39; Deut. 16:3).

The plague on the firstborn was destined to "bring judgment on all the gods of Egypt" (v. 12), some of whom had already been judged individually by the preceding nine plagues. Moses' father-in-law, Jethro, would soon confess his faith in the supremacy of the Lord over "all other gods" (18:11) after hearing of what the Lord had done to the Egyptians—including the pharaoh's firstborn, whom the Egyptians believed to be a god.

The Passover was to be celebrated on the fourteenth of Abib and combined with the Feast of Unleavened Bread, which was to be observed "from the evening of the fourteenth day until the evening of the twenty-first day" (vv. 17-18). During that entire week nothing made with yeast was to be eaten (vv. 19-20). As for the blood of the Passover lamb, "a bunch of hyssop" (v. 22) was the instrument used to daub it on the doorframes of the houses. Hyssop (*Origanum maru*) is an aromatic plant of the mint family, with a straight stalk (John 19:29), a humble plant that even today "grows out of walls" (1 Kings 4:33). The hairy surface of its leaves and branches holds liquids well and makes it suitable as a sprinkling device for purification rituals (Lev. 14:4, 6, 49, 51-52; Num. 19:6, 18; Psalm 51:7; Heb. 9:19).

"The destroyer" (v. 23) was the angel assigned to carry out the Lord's judgment of the plague on the firstborn of Egypt. Destructive plagues were often brought through angels sent by God (2 Sam. 24:15-16; 2 Kings 19:35; Ps. 78:49; see also 1 Cor. 10:10, a reference to Num. 16:41-49). The connection between the word "Passover" and the fact that the Lord "passed over" the houses of the Israelites is made explicit in verse 27.

The people of Israel were to celebrate the Feasts of Passover and Unleavened Bread (for all practical purposes, combined as one feast; see Mark 14:1, 12) for all future generations. They were to commemorate it (v. 14; 13:3), celebrate it (v. 17), obey its instructions (v. 24), observe it (v. 25), remind their children of its meaning (vv. 26-27; 13:8, 14-15), keep it on their minds and lips, in their thoughts and hands (13:9, 16), remember it (Deut. 16:3)—for all future generations. Passover would forever commemorate their deliverance from Egypt, and Unleavened Bread would remind them of the hardships of their hurried flight.

In obedience to God's command, the Passover Feast was observed often in biblical times (Num. 9:1-5; Josh. 5:10; 2 Kings 23:21-23; 2 Chron. 30:1-27; Ezra 6:19-22; Luke 2:41-43; John 2:13, 23; 6:4; 11:55—12:1) and is still kept by most Jewish families today. Every such family conducts a *Seder* ("order of service") annually on the evenings of the fourteenth and fifteenth of Nisan. Before the first of the two Seders the house is systematically (often only symbolically) searched to make sure not a crumb of leavened bread is present (see Exod. 12:15, 19). In the New Testament, "yeast" frequently symbolizes sin (Luke 12:1; 1 Cor. 5:8).

The ceremony of *Kiddush* ("sanctification"), which begins the Seder itself, proclaims the holiness of the day by pronouncing a benediction over wine. The person conducting the Seder, usually the father of the household, then has water ritually poured over his hands. Next the officiant dips a sprig of parsley or other plant in salt water (compare Exod. 12:22) to symbolize the meager diet and tears of the Israelites under Egyptian oppression. He then breaks one of three pieces of *matzah* ("unleavened bread") earlier placed under cover on the table. The larger part of the broken piece is wrapped in a napkin and hidden for later use. Next comes the recital of the Passover story, which includes answers to four questions asked by the youngest child present (compare 12:26-27; 13:8, 14-15). Then everyone performs the ritual washing of the hands and recites the usual blessing customary before every meal. The traditional benediction is recited, followed by a special blessing for the matzah.

Next each person eats two pieces of matzah broken off from two of the three pieces under cover. Then everyone eats bitter herbs (see 12:8), a reminder of the bitterness of their ancestors' slavery (1:13-14). The herbs are first dipped in *haroseth,* a mixture of apples, nuts, raisins, cinnamon, and wine, to symbolize the mortar (1:14) used in building store cities for the pharaoh (1:11).

That is followed by the festive holiday meal itself, which usually begins with an egg dipped in salt water as a symbolic reminder of the destruction of Herod's Temple. (The practice of dipping eggs in food coloring during the Easter season is believed to originate from that ritual.) The hidden half matzah is then eaten. Finally, the Seder concludes with prayers and songs of thanksgiving, praise, and rejoicing.

And so it is that Jews down through the centuries have elaborated upon the simple ceremony of Exodus 12, adding some items and subtracting others. But they have not forgotten that the Passover commemorates their release from slavery in Egypt, even though the sacrificial aspect of the ceremony has been lost (partly for practical reasons). Although one of the items in their holiday meal is a roasted shank bone, reminiscent of the eating of the Passover lamb (vv. 8-11), all Jewish sacrifices came to an end in A.D. 70 when the Roman armies destroyed Herod's Temple, demolished the sacrificial altar, and dispersed the Jews of Jerusalem throughout the then-known world.

Only one small group of people, known as the Samaritans and numbering just a few hundred, still celebrate Passover essentially as it was observed in biblical times. Living for the most part in Nablus in the shadow of Mount Gerizim in central Israel, they claim to be the surviving remnant of the ancient Israelites. Each spring they keep the Passover on the fourteenth of Nisan and observe the details in Exodus 12 virtually to the letter, including the sacrifice of lambs.

Jesus, an observant Jew Himself, celebrated the Passover annually in Jerusalem whenever possible (Luke 2:41-43; John 2:13, 23; 12:1), although on at least one occasion He may have stayed in the region of Galilee during that time (6:1-14). The accounts of the Last Supper in the New Testament indicate that Jesus and His disciples participated in a Passover observance very similar to the form kept by Jews today. The Passover lamb that our Lord and His disciples ate was sacrificed on the "first day of the Feast of Unleavened Bread" (Mark 14:12). The gospel narratives mention dipping food into a bowl (Matt. 26:23; Mark 14:20) or dish (John 13:26). The bread that Jesus broke, the bread that represents His body broken for us (Mark 14:22), was probably the hidden half matzah eaten near the end of the meal.

As for the cup that He passed around to His disciples, an additional bit of information related to current practice provides the clue for understanding it. Jews who celebrate the Passover today always reserve a place of honor at the table for the possible coming of Elijah (which they claim will fulfill Malachi 4:5). A special cup, or chalice, also reserved for him, is filled with wine at a particular time during the meal. No one drinks it, and it is disposed of after the ceremony. Paul tells us that "after supper" (1 Cor. 11:25) Jesus took the cup. By that time all the other cups were empty, so Jesus must have passed to His disciples the cup filled and reserved for Elijah—the cup from which no one ever drank. Jesus was therefore proclaiming that He Himself was the long-awaited Messiah and that the cup represented the new covenant in His blood.

By breaking the bread and sharing the cup, and by telling the disciples what both acts symbolized, Jesus transformed the Last Supper into the Lord's Supper. As observant Jews still celebrate the Passover as a reminder of their national redemption from Egyptian bondage (Exod. 13:3), so Christians celebrate Communion as a reminder of their spiritual redemption from bondage to sin—redemption that was purchased by the broken body and shed blood of Jesus Christ (1 Cor. 11:24-26).

Before the Jewish Seder can begin, the home must be cleansed of all its old bread crumbs. Before Holy Communion can begin for us, we must examine ourselves (1 Cor. 11:28) and "get rid of the old yeast" (5:7), because "Christ, our Passover Lamb, has been sacrificed" (5:7) once for all time (Heb. 7:27). After the Jewish Seder is over, songs of thanksgiving and praise are sung. After the institution of Holy Communion, Jesus and His disciples sang a hymn (Mark 14:26), a practice still followed today. After Jesus cleanses our hearts, we too can sing.

Passover: Regulations (12:43-49). Since the Passover was being instituted for the specific purpose of helping the Israelites remember that God had delivered them from slavery, foreigners (including temporary residents and hired workers) would not be permitted to share in it (vv. 43, 45). Purchased slaves, as well as aliens living among the Israelites, could partake, but only after being circumcised (vv. 44, 48). Only in the most unusual circumstances (see, for example, 2 Chron. 30:15-20) did the Lord accept any deviation from restrictions such as those. Ritual and spiritual purity were prerequisites for eating the Passover (Exod. 12:48), just as spiritual purity is required of all who partake of the Lord's Supper (1 Cor. 11:28).

None of the meat of the Passover lamb was to be taken out of the house, and none of the bones was to be broken (Exod. 12:46; Num. 9:12). Psalm 34:19-20 tells about a righteous man whom the Lord delivers from all his troubles so that none of his bones is broken. The soldiers who nailed our Passover Lamb (1 Cor. 5:7) to the cross returned later to break the legs of the criminals hanging beside Jesus in order to hasten their death. But when they noticed that Jesus was already dead, the soldiers did not break His legs, and so the Old Testament passages were fulfilled (John 19:31-33, 36).

Passover: Consecration of firstborn (12:50—13:16). Because God had adopted Israel as His firstborn son (Exod. 4:22) and brought him out of Egypt (Hos. 11:1), the first off-spring of every womb among the Israelites, whether man or animal, belongs to Him (Exod. 13:2). Every Israelite firstborn is also to be consecrated to Him because the Lord killed every Egyptian firstborn in order to force the pharaoh to free the Israelites (v. 15) and because He delivered every Israelite from the tenth plague (12:12-13). The economic importance of donkeys as pack animals allowed for their redemption through the sacrifice of a lamb (13:13).

Although human sacrifice was a widespread practice in the ancient world, it was absolutely forbidden among the Israelites. The consecration of firstborn Israelite sons is therefore to be accomplished through making an appropriate token payment (see for example Num. 3:39-51). In verse 13 ("Redeem every firstborn among your sons"), then, the verb "redeem" has its most basic meaning: "buy back at a price." Jesus, the virgin Mary's firstborn son (Luke 2:7), was brought to Jerusalem and presented to the Lord at the appropriate time. Joseph and Mary brought Him in accordance with the divine command of Exodus 13:2, 12, which is stated to be both a part of the "Law of Moses" (Luke 2:22) and the "Law of the Lord" (2:23). The law of Moses is therefore claimed to have God as its ultimate source, a clear testimony to its divine inspiration.

The celebration of Passover and the Feast of Unleavened Bread would serve to remind the Israelites annually (v. 10) that the Lord had delivered them from Egyptian slavery. But the Exodus redemption would become the most significant and memorable spiritual experience in Israel's national history, and so it needed to be brought to mind far more often than merely once as year. One should be able to describe the Exodus and its observance as "as sign on your hand and a reminder on your forehead" (v. 9) or as "as symbol on your forehead" (v. 16). The commands, the laws, the decrees, the requirements of the Lord soon to be revealed to Israel should be joyfully welcomed by God's people under a similar divine imperative: "Tie them as symbols on your hands and bind them on your foreheads" (Deut. 6:8; 11:18).

For two thousand years and more, observant Jews have taken those passages literally. The paragraphs that form their contexts (Exod. 13:1-10; 13:11-16; Deut. 6:4-9; 11:13-21) are written on four strips of parchment and placed in two small leather boxes, one of which the pious Jewish man straps on his forehead and the other on his left arm before he says his morning prayers. The practice may have originated as early as the period following the exile to Babylon in 586 B.C.

It hardly needs to be said that there is nothing inherently wrong with such a custom. The boxes, called "phylacteries," are mentioned in Matthew 23:5, where Jesus criticizes a certain group of Pharisees and teachers of the law for wearing them. Our Lord, however, condemns not the practice as such but the ostentatious use of "wide" phylacteries as part of a general statement about those who flaunt their religiosity in public: "Everything they do is done for men to see."

But although the proper and modest use of phylacteries might be spiritually legitimate, it is probably best to understand the references from Exodus and Deuteronomy as figures of speech, since similar statements are found elsewhere in the Old Testament. For example, of love and faithfulness it is said, "Bind them around your neck, write them on the tablet of your heart" (Prov. 3:3), and, even more to the point, of a father's commands and a mother's teaching it is suggested, "Bind them upon your heart forever; fasten them around your neck" (6:21; see also 7:3; Song of Sol. 8:6). Perhaps the explanation of Deuteronomy 11:18 says it best: "Fix these words of mine in your hearts and minds." For all but the most spiritually sensitive, it can be a cause for misunderstanding to wear religion on one's sleeve.

7

REDEMPTION

EXODUS 12:31-42; 13:17—15:21

We have now come to the middle chapter of this commentary, and it is providential that we have also reached the portion of the book of Exodus that tells the story of the Exodus itself—the central theme of the book. When God freed His people from slavery in Egypt, His "mighty hand" (Exod. 6:1) and "outstretched arm" (6:6) performed the greatest act of redemption in the Old Testament period. German scholars affirm its importance when they refer to the Old Testament as *Heilsgeschichte,* which means "history of salvation." Just as the redemption brought about by the crucifixion and resurrection of Jesus Christ constitutes the main theme of the New Testament, so the redemption brought about by God's "mighty acts of judgment" (7:4) at the time of the Exodus constitutes the main theme not only of the book of Exodus but of the entire Old Testament as well.

Old Testament redemption and New Testament redemption are not identical, of course. The Exodus redemption was basically national and corporate, whereas the redemption effected by Jesus' death on Calvary is basically individual and personal. Old Testament redemption at the time of the Exodus was primarily physical and political, whereas New Testament redemption is primarily (though not totally) spiritual. But the similarities between the two are striking indeed. In both cases death was the terrible price necessary to bring about redemption, in both cases the specific redemptive act became the most important event in the history of God's people, and in both cases the redemptive event is periodically celebrated by means of a joyful ceremony having its origin in the Passover meal.

Before proceeding to the story of the stupendous miracle at the Sea of Reeds, we will turn back to consider briefly Exodus 12:31-42, a passage outlining the first stage of Israel's escape from Egyptian bondage.

Freedom at last (12:31-42). The Israelites left the store city of Rameses (v. 37) "on the fifteenth day of the first month, the day after the Passover" (Num. 33:3). During the previous night, however, "Pharaoh summoned Moses and Aaron" (v. 31), either by retracting his rash vow that Moses would never see him again (10:28) or by sending representatives. His unconditional release of all the Israelites and their possessions was a long time in coming, but it was God's predetermined response (11:1) to the frequent earlier pleas of Moses: "Let my people go" (5:1; 7:16; 8:1, 20; 9:1, 13; 10:3). The pharaoh concluded his frantic speech to Moses and Aaron by saying to them, "And also bless me" (v. 32)—a humble request for a proud ruler who up till then had ignored God persistently and completely.

The Egyptians agreed with the pharaoh's decision to free Israel. They had witnessed the death of their firstborn, and they feared for their own lives as well (v. 33). They were even willing to be "plundered" (v. 36; see 3:22) by the Israelites if that would hasten their departure. The verb "plunder" is used here only as a vivid figure of speech, however, since the Israelites had simply "asked" (v. 35; see also 3:22; 11:2) the Egyptians for certain kinds of items and since the Lord had made the Egyptians "favorably disposed" (v. 36; 3:21; 11:3) toward the people of Israel. The circumstances recorded here were later celebrated and set to music (Ps. 105:37-38). Israel herself was to follow the same principle of providing gifts for released slaves (Deut. 15:12-15).

At long last, after successive generations of Israelites had lived 430 years in Egypt (vv. 40-41), the people began their

epic migration back to Canaan. During the time of the
patriarchs the Lord had told Abram that his descendants
would be "strangers in a country not their own" and that
they would be "enslaved and mistreated four hundred years"
(Gen. 15:13) but that "in the fourth generation" (15:16) they
would return to their homeland. Since a generation in
Abram's case would have been one hundred years—his age
when Isaac was born (21:5)—the figures in Genesis 15 may be
intended as round numbers for the "430" in Exodus 12:40-41
(see also Acts 7:6; 13:17-20; Gal. 3:17).

Leaving Rameses (location uncertain), the Israelites arrived
at Succoth (v. 37), probably the same as modern Tell el-
Maskhutah in the eastern delta region. They numbered
"about six hundred thousand men on foot, besides women
and children." After their arrival at Mount Sinai, we read,
the men numbered "603,550" (38:26). How are we to understand such a huge figure, which must be raised to from two to
three million when the women and children are included?

Humanly speaking, enormous problems are involved. That
seventy people (1:5) could multiply to three million in 430
years presents no difficulty, because it can be shown through
simple mathematics that if each Israelite couple produced
only five or six children (not a large family in those days) who
lived to a marriageable age the resulting population would
have approached four million within four hundred years—
especially in the ideal climate and lush farmlands and pastures
of Goshen. The book of Exodus itself states that "the
Israelites were fruitful and multiplied greatly and became ex-
ceedingly numerous, so that the land was filled with them"
(1:7).

Problems arise, however, when we remember that the people would be walking through Sinai, a "vast and dreadful
desert" (Deut. 1:19; 8:15), "that thirsty and waterless land"
(8:15), and that they would therefore need large quantities of
food and water. In addition, the logistics of such a journey
for so many people would be almost insurmountable: insur-

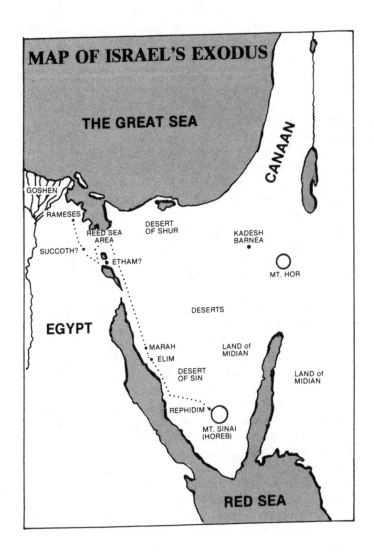

MAP OF ISRAEL'S EXODUS

THE GREAT SEA

CANAAN

GOSHEN

RAMESES

REED SEA AREA

DESERT OF SHUR

KADESH BARNEA

SUCCOTH?

ETHAM?

MT. HOR

EGYPT

DESERTS

MARAH

ELIM

LAND of MIDIAN

DESERT OF SIN

LAND of MIDIAN

REPHIDIM

MT. SINAI (HOREB)

RED SEA

ing protection from bandits and wild animals, supplying clothing and shelter, providing medical care, mediating disputes—the list goes on and on.

Faced with such difficulties, many Bible students have tried to drastically reduce the number *603,550* in various ways: by interpreting it nonliterally, by assuming that it represents a later census figure read back into the Exodus story, or by translating the Hebrew word for "thousand" as "clan" (as is sometimes legitimately done—in 1 Sam. 23:23, for example) or "(military) unit" (see, for example, 1 Sam. 17:18). All such well-meaning proposals are attempts to bring the number down to manageable proportions (in the tens of thousands at most) in order to save the credibility of the Exodus narrative.

But the figure "603,550" is found not only in Exodus 38:26 but also in Numbers 1:46, where it represents the exact total of the numbers of men in each of the twelve Israelite tribes as tabulated in Numbers 1. In addition, "603,550" appears in Numbers 2:32, where it functions as in 1:46—but this time Numbers 2 lists not only the numbers of men in each of the twelve tribes but also groups the tribes into four sets of three tribes each and then gives subtotals for the number of men in each set. In other words, the book of Numbers takes pains to indicate that the number "603,550" should be understood literally and that "thousand" cannot mean "clan" or "(military) unit" in Numbers 1-2. It is also highly unlikely that Numbers intends for us to interpret the figures as insertions from a later census since it uses them in a specific and detailed historical context.

It would seem, then, that the number in Exodus 38:26 should be understood literally and that "six hundred thousand" (12:37) is a legitimate approximation of it. Although the number is admittedly huge, it is not impossibly large and compares favorably with similar figures in the books of Judges through 2 Chronicles. We observe also that the books of Exodus and Numbers continually emphasize that God was supernaturally providing for His people and protecting them on their journey through the Sinai desert. The resources of an omnipotent and loving God can just as easily supply the needs of a few million people as of a few thousand.

"Many other people" (Exod. 12:38) shared Israel's blessing by leaving Egypt with them, possibly including Egyptians such as those "who feared the word of the LORD" (9:20). No doubt malcontents from other lands (like the "rabble" of Num. 11:4) also seized the opportunity to flee from the pharaoh.

B. THE MIRACLE AT THE SEA OF REEDS (13:17—15:21)

The fugitives, including Moses and Aaron, were probably unaware of and unprepared for the mighty miracle that God was about to perform for their deliverance.

1. *Crossing the Sea* (13:17—14:31). Northern, middle, and southern routes have all been suggested as possible ways along which the people might have traveled through the Sinai desert toward Canaan. But the central route is almost impossible to coordinate with the biblical names of the places where the Israelites camped, and the northern route was forbidden by God Himself because, although it was the shortest and therefore the most direct, it was heavily guarded by a line of Egyptian fortresses that would surely have forced the people to return to Egypt (v. 17). So the Lord led them "around by the desert road" (v. 18), which probably eventually turned south along the west coast of the Sinai peninsula before winding its way toward the interior in a southeasterly direction.

The phrase "Red Sea" means literally "Sea of Reeds," using the same Hebrew word for "reeds" as is found in 2:3. "Sea of Reeds" might be a common noun rather than a proper name and could therefore refer to more than one body of water, depending on context. It is used of the Red Sea in 1 Kings 9:26, but we can be fairly certain that a different body

of water was the location of the miraculous crossing of the
Sea of Reeds in Exodus.[1] Many sites have been proposed not
far from the line followed by the modern Suez Canal (Lake
Timsah or the Bitter Lakes, for example), and bodies of water
farther to the north (such as Lake Sirbonis near the Mediterranean) have also been suggested. The Red Sea itself (including its western arm, the Gulf of Suez) would appear to be
too far south to fit the detailed description of Exodus 14:2.

The Lord had told Abraham that his descendants would
leave Egypt and return to Canaan (Gen. 15:13-16).
Abraham's great-grandson Joseph believed that promise
(50:24), and he made his brothers take an oath that they or
their descendants would carry his bones with them when they
made the journey (50:25). Moses, in recognition of Joseph's
faith (Heb. 11:22), fulfilled his dying wish (Exod. 13:19).
Since Moses died at the borders of the Promised Land, the
Israelites who later entered Canaan took Joseph's bones with
them and buried them at Shechem (Josh. 24:32). The traditional tomb of Joseph can be visited near the ancient site of
Shechem today.

Leaving Succoth, the people camped at Etham (v. 20; exact
location unknown, although the word is Egyptian and means
"Fortress Wall"). The Lord continued to lead His people
along by a pillar of cloud by day and a pillar of fire by night
(v. 21). There was only one pillar rather than two (see the
phrase "pillar of fire and cloud" in 14:24), so perhaps the
word "cloud" is a picturesque way of referring to the smoke
of the fire.

Like the burning bush (3:2), the pillar was the visible symbol of God's presence among His people. The Lord Himself
was in the pillar (13:21; 14:24) and often spoke to the people
from it (Num. 12:5-6; Deut. 31:15-16; Ps. 99:6-7). The later
hymn-writers of Israel fondly remembered it (Pss. 78:14;

---

1. Merrill F. Unger, *Unger's Bible Dictionary* (Chicago: Moody, 1957), p.
331.

105:39). A similar cloud of smoke came to represent the glory of the Lord in the sanctuary throughout much of Israel's history (Exod. 40:34-35; 1 Kings 8:10-11; Isa. 4:5; 6:3-4). Our God never leaves His people without the guidance they need.

The Lord then told Moses to command the Israelites to "turn back" (Exod. 14:2)—that is, northward (the general direction from which they had come). They were to camp "near Pi Hahiroth," which is located "east of Baal Zephon" (Num. 33:7). The latter phrase means "Baal of the North," the Canaanite god after whom the town was named. "Migdol" (location unknown) is a Semitic word meaning "Watchtower," and the "sea" in Exodus 14:2 is the Sea of Reeds. An Egyptian papyrus associates Baal Zephon with Tahpahnes (Jer. 2:16; 43:7-9; 44:1; 46:14; Ezek. 30:18), a known site near Lake Menzaleh in the northeastern delta region. Lake Menzaleh is therefore the most likely candidate for the Sea of Reeds, and the crossing of the Sea probably took place near its southern end.

Realizing that they had lost an irreplaceable supply of cheap labor, the pharaoh and his officials changed their minds and pursued the fugitives (vv. 5-6). All the chariots of Egypt (v. 7) would be needed to chase down such an enormous number of escapees. The chariots were manned by "officers" (v. 7), the singular form of which means in Hebrew "third man" (perhaps referring to his relative position in a chariot). The Israelites, terrified by the approaching Egyptians, said to Moses, "Was it because there were no graves in Egypt that you brought us to the desert to die?" (v. 11). Their cry contained a heavy dose of sarcasm, since through most of her recorded history Egypt had been a land of tombs and sepulchers.

Moses' response to Israel was twofold: "Do not be afraid" (v. 13), a word of encouragement from God that had earlier been given to Abraham (Gen. 15:1) and Isaac (26:24) and that would later be given to Joshua (Josh. 8:1), and "The LORD will fight for you" (v. 14; see also 15:3; Neh. 4:20; Ps. 35:1), a needed reminder that although Israel was "armed for battle" (Exod. 13:18) and "marching out boldly" (14:8), the victory would be won by God alone.

The angel of God and the pillar of cloud then moved from in front of Israel's army and took up positions behind it, "coming between the armies of Egypt and Israel" (vv. 19-20) in order to protect God's people (Ps. 105:39). Then the Lord drove the sea back with a strong east wind (v. 21; see also 10:13), referred to poetically as the blast of God's nostrils (15:8) and stressing once again that miracles issue from God and occur in accordance with His timing as He controls the forces of nature to accomplish His will. The Israelites were able to go through the sea "on dry ground" (v. 22), a fact marveled at by later psalmists and prophets (Pss. 66:6; 106:9; Isa. 51:10; 63:11-13). A "wall of water" (v. 22; Ps. 78:13) flanked the people of God on their right and on their left—water that "piled up" and "congealed" (Exod. 15:8).

At the time of "the morning watch" (v. 24), during the "last watch of the night" (1 Sam. 11:11) just before "daybreak" (see v. 27), the Lord threw the Egyptian army into confusion and made it difficult for them to drive their chariots (vv. 24-25). He then caused the waters to flow back to their place and swept the Egyptians into the Sea (vv. 26-27), just as He had done with the locusts of the eighth plague (10:19). "The entire army of Pharaoh" (v. 28) drowned in the deep waters, and not one of his charioteers survived.[2]

The Lord's victory was complete, and the evidence of it was visible: The Israelites saw "the Egyptians lying dead on the shore" (v. 30). But, more important, they saw also the almighty hand of the Lord Himself at work, so they expressed

---

2. Although Psalm 136:15 states that God "swept Pharaoh and his army into the Red Sea," it is not necessary to assume that the pharaoh himself personally died of drowning along with his charioteers. See, for example, Howard F. Vos, *Archaeology in Bible Lands* (Chicago: Moody, 1977), p. 241. The phrase "Pharaoh and his army" may be a figure of speech for "Pharaoh's army."

their faith in God's power and confidence in Moses' leadership (v. 31). It is worth noting here that leaders of men must be servants of men and of God, as were Caleb (Num. 14:24), Joshua (Josh. 24:29), Samuel (1 Sam. 3:10), David (2 Sam. 3:18), Elijah (2 Kings 9:36), and, supremely, Moses himself (Exod. 14:31; Deut. 34:5). When Moses raised his staff over the Sea (v. 16) he was not trying to perform a trick with a magic wand. The Lord was working through His servant, and the mighty power of God Himself was in Moses' staff (see Isa. 10:26).

2. *A hymn of victory* (15:1-21). The miracle at the Sea of Reeds, God's greatest act of redemption during the Old Testament period, is described not only in narrative prose (Exod. 13:17—14:31) but also in lyric poetry (15:1-21). And it is fitting indeed that the Song of Miriam (see vv. 20-21), so called to differentiate it from the Song of Moses (Deut. 31:30—32:43), is considered by many scholars to be one of the oldest poems, if not the oldest[3], in the Bible, contemporary with the miraculous event it celebrates.

As in the prose account, so also in the poetic hymn: The focus of the story is on God Himself (v. 11); the name "LORD" appears ten times (vv. 1, 2, 3*a*, 3*b*, 6*a*, 6*b*, 11, 16, 17*c*, 18; "Lord" in 17*d* is the less intimate word *Adonay*). The hymn contains five stanzas (vv. 1-5, 6-8, 9-10, 11-12, 13-18), each of the first three of which concludes with a simile ("like a stone," v. 5; "like a wall," v. 8; "like lead," v. 10). The first four stanzas tell the story of the deliverance of Israel at the Sea of Reeds, and the final stanza predicts the conquest of Canaan.

The phrase "I will sing" (v. 1) frequently begins hymns of victory and praise in the Bible (Judg. 5:3; Pss. 89:1; 101:1; 108:1) as well as in Canaanite literature. The first half of verse 2 is quoted verbatim in Psalm 118:14. There, as here, the

---

3. William F. Albright, *Yahweh and the Gods of Canaan* (Garden City, N.Y.: Doubleday, 1968), pp. 12-13.

word "song" may also be translated "defender." The imagery of sinking like a stone (v. 5) is applied also to Babylon, another of Israel's enemies, in Jeremiah 51:63-64.

As the blast of God's nostrils piled the waters up (v. 8), so also He blew with His breath to bring the waters back (v. 10). Both are powerful figures of speech that describe the mighty winds used by God to control the waters, the first time to rescue His people and the second time to destroy their enemies.

The rhetorical question "Who is like you?" (v. 11; see also Pss. 35:10; 71:19; 89:6; 113:5; Mic. 7:18) drives home the point that God, who brooks no rivals, is the one who has defeated the gods of Egypt (see also 12:12) and their worshipers. Since it was actually the Sea that swallowed up the Egyptians, the word "earth" (v. 12) probably refers to Sheol or the grave (Pss. 63:9; 71:20), the "realm of death below" (Deut. 32:22).

God's "holy dwelling" (v. 13) would be built first at Shiloh in central Canaan (Jer. 7:12) but would eventually be the Temple in Jerusalem (Ps. 76:2), the "place" God would "choose" (Deut. 12:14, 18, 26; 14:25; 16:7, 15-16; 17:8, 10; 18:6; 31:11) to put "his Name" (Deut. 12:5, 11, 21; 14:23-24; 16:2, 6, 11; 26:2). The nations named in verses 14-15 are listed roughly in the order along the route that Israel would eventually follow on their way to the Promised Land. The term "chiefs" (v. 15) was used earlier of Edomite rulers in Genesis 36. The fact that "the LORD will reign for ever and ever" reminds us that God is called the King of His people in two other poems roughly contemporary with the Song of Miriam (see Num. 23:21; Deut. 33:5).

Concerned about her brother Moses soon after his birth (Exod. 2:4, 7-8), Miriam now sang her song and led a group of women "with tambourines and dancing" (v. 20). Such celebration was common after victory in battle (1 Sam. 18:6), and the prophetic gift, which Miriam rightly (if jealously) claimed to have (Num. 12:1-2), was often accompanied by the use of music (1 Sam. 10:5). Other prophetesses in Israel were Deborah (Judg. 4:4), Isaiah's wife (Isa. 8:3), Huldah (2 Kings 22:14), Noadiah (Neh. 6:14), and Anna (Luke 2:36).

The French princess Eugénie's toast at the cutting of the Suez Canal near the end of the nineteenth century was as follows: "Thirty-five centuries ago, the waters of the Red Sea drew back at the word of Moses. Today, at the order of the sovereign of Egypt they return to their bed.[4] Although the princess Eugénie gave far too much credit to the role of human activity in the moving of the waters in both ancient and modern times, the prophetess Miriam gave full glory to the Lord, who is "highly exalted" (v. 21).

---

4. Quoted in *Aramco World,* September-October, 1975, p. 9.

8

JOURNEY

C. FROM THE SEA OF REEDS TO SINAI (15:22—18:27)

The most common response to God's gift of redemption is a spontaneous outburst of gratitude and joy. As one might have expected, Moses and the Israelites reacted in just that way by singing a hymn of victory to the Lord who had redeemed them (15:1), and the prophetess Miriam did the same (v. 21).

But redemption is the beginning, not the end, of a journey. And although life after redemption is usually challenging and exciting at first, all too quickly it can become tedious and boring—especially if we forget and forsake our first love (Rev. 2:4). When that takes place, grumbling and complaining against the Lord and His leaders is not far behind. Unfortunately the Israelites, who had so recently experienced the greatest act of redemption that would ever take place in their long history as a nation, were about to embark on a life of defeat by forgetting the Lord and dwelling on their problems.

1. *The first crisis: Thirst* (15:22-27). Leaving the Sea of Reeds, the people went into the desert of "Shur" (v. 22), located east of Egypt (Gen. 25:18; 1 Sam. 15:7) in the northwestern part of Sinai. The same region is called the "Desert of Etham" in Numbers 33:8. ("Shur" and "Etham" both mean "Fortress Wall," *Shur* being a Hebrew word and *Etham* its Egyptian equivalent.)

Although recent Israeli geological surveys have demon-

strated that there may be huge underground reservoirs of
fresh water in the Sinai peninsula, oases on the surface of the
ground have always been few and widely scattered. After
traveling for several days without finding water fit to drink,
the people of Israel grumbled against Moses (v. 24). In so doing they set in motion a pattern that would be repeated whenever they faced a crisis (16:2; 17:3; Num. 14:2; 16:11, 41). At
a more profound level, of course, their grumbling was not
against Moses and Aaron alone but "against the LORD"
(Exod. 16:8) as well (see also Ps. 106:25), and Paul warns us
not to follow their example (1 Cor. 10:10).

One of the places where the water was too brackish to drink
was called "Marah" (v. 23), which means "Bitter." It should
probably be identified with modern Ain Hawarah, east of the
Gulf of Suez about fifty miles south of its northern end. The
"piece of wood" that Moses threw into the water to sweeten
it may have been part of an aromatic plant, the effects of
which were miraculously heightened by God. A similar
miraculous "healing" of water is described in 2 Kings
2:19-22.

Long before the formal giving of the law on Mount Sinai,
God's people were expected to keep certain commands,
decrees, and regulations given to them at various times (Gen.
26:5) as well as to conduct themselves generally in ways that
were "right and just" (Gen. 18:19). We should not be surprised, then, that the Lord demanded obedience to "a decree
and a law" that He made for them at Marah (vv. 25-26). As
then (v. 25), God often tests His people by means of such
commands (20:20). He would soon test the Israelites also in
connection with His provision of manna for them (16:4), in-
tending to strengthen their faith and ultimately to increase
their joy (Deut. 8:16).

The "healing" of the waters at Marah, together with the
promise of continued good health for His people, was the
occasion for God to reveal one of His many compound titles
formed by combining the personal name *Yahweh* with

another element, in this case *Yahweh Rophe,* "The LORD Who Heals" (v. 26). Other examples, given in equally solemn contexts, are *Yahweh Yir'eh,* "The LORD Will Provide" (Gen. 22:14); *Yahweh Nissi,* "The LORD Is My Banner" (Exod. 17:15); *Yahweh Shalom,* "The LORD Is Peace" (Judg. 6:24); *Yahweh Ro'i,* "The LORD Is My Shepherd" (Ps. 23:1); *Yahweh Tsidqenu,* "The LORD Our Righteouness" (Jer. 23:6); and *Yahweh Shammah,* "The LORD Is There" (Ezek. 48:35). All such names for God emphasize that *Yahweh* is the One who enters into personal and intimate relationships with His people. The title of one of Francis Schaeffer's books well expresses that basic idea: *He Is There and He Is Not Silent.*

Continuing on their journey, the Israelites traveled seven miles south of Marah and camped at Elim in the well-watered valley today called Wadi Gharandel. There, as the eyewitness who wrote the account tells us, they found "twelve springs and seventy palm trees" (v. 27). *Elim* means "large trees" in Hebrew.

2. *The second crisis: Hunger* (16:1-36). Departing from Elim, the people came to the desert of "Sin" (a proper name probably derived from "Sinai," the meaning of which is unknown). The region was in southwestern Sinai in the area today called Debbet er-Ramleh. The Israelites arrived there exactly one month after their exodus from Egypt (v. 1; see 12:2, 6, 29, 31). No sooner did they settle down in their tents than they began to complain of hunger. They remembered the "pots of meat" (doubtless an exaggeration) and other "food" (v. 3) they had in Egypt, such as fish, cucumbers, melons, leeks, onions, and garlic (Num. 11:5).

The Lord, ever gracious toward His people, told Moses that He would rain down "bread from heaven" (v. 4), bread that would be remembered and celebrated in later generations (Neh. 9:15; Pss. 78:24-25; 105:40; John 6:31). God told the Israelites that they were to go out each day and gather just enough bread for that day (v. 4), a command that probably underlies Jesus' model petition: "Give us each day our daily bread" (Luke 11:3; see also Matt. 6:11). On the sixth day they were to gather twice as much as on any of the other days (v. 5) in order to provide for "the seventh day, the Sabbath" (v. 26), "a day of rest" (v. 23).

The bread would be supplied for their morning needs, whereas in the evenings they would eat meat (vv. 8, 12) in the form of quail (v. 13). A similar but different provision of quail for the people's needs is described in Numbers 11:31-33. As for the bread, it came with the morning dew and appeared as "thin flakes like frost" on the desert floor (v. 14). It was "white like coriander seed" (v. 31) and "looked like resin" (Num. 11:7). It tasted like "wafers made with honey" (v. 31), like "something made with olive oil" (Num. 11:8). Never having seen it before and therefore not knowing what it was, the Israelites called it *manna* (v. 31), a Semitic word meaning "What is it?" (see v. 15).

Such detailed descriptions make it possible that the biblical manna is to be identified with the sticky and often granular honeydew that is excreted in the Sinai peninsula in the late spring by various scale insects. It solidifies rapidly through evaporation and is still collected and called "manna" or "man" by people living in Sinai and other dry regions of the Middle East.[1] God's miraculous provision for His people would then have consisted in multiplying it in large enough quantities for His people's needs and bringing it to them at just the right time, while making it totally unavailable to them every seventh day (vv. 25-27).

Whether we should even look for a partially natural explanation for the manna is not nearly as important, however, as the lesson to be learned from God's selective provision of it: The Lord reminded Israel that the principle of the seventh

1. F. S. Bodenheimer "The Manna of Sinai," in *The Biblical Archaeologist Reader,* ed. G. Ernest Wright and David N. Freedman (Garden City, N.Y.: Doubleday, 1961), pp. 76-80.

day as a day of rest and holiness had been established after He created the heavens and the earth (the Hebrew verb translated "rested" in Gen. 2:2-3 is the origin of the noun "Sabbath," which appears for the first time in Exod. 16:23). The Israelites would be commanded in 20:8-11 to work six days and rest on the seventh because that is what God did.

Manna as "bread from heaven" (v. 4) prefigures the coming of Jesus as "the true bread from heaven" (John 6:32), "the bread of God" (6:33), "the living bread that came down from heaven" (6:51)—all in a spiritual sense (6:63). Jesus, as both the "bread of life" (6:35, 48) and the source of the "water of life" (Rev. 21:6; 22:1, 17), can therefore say to us, "He who comes to me will never go hungry, and he who believes in me will never be thirsty" (John 6:35). Jesus makes the contrast between manna and Himself explicit in John 6:58: "Our forefathers ate manna and died, but he who feeds on this bread will live forever." We gain that glorious life by believing in Him (6:40).

Another typological application of the Old Testament account of the manna is found in the Old Testament itself. We are told that the Lord gave His people manna to teach them that "man does not live on bread alone but on every word that comes from the mouth of the LORD" (Deut. 8:3). At the beginning of His ministry Jesus made good use of that text when the devil tempted Him with hunger in the desert (Matt. 4:1-4; Luke 4:1-4). In so doing He illustrated the important fact that spiritual nourishment is equally as significant as physical satisfaction.

Since the physical needs of the Israelites in the Desert of Sin had to be met, they each gathered an average of one "omer" (about two quarts) of manna a day (v. 16). "He who gathered much did not have too much, and he who gathered little did not have too little" (v. 18) describes a historical situation cited verbatim by Paul as an illustration of Christians who share with each other what they possess (2 Cor. 8:15). By contrast, the greed of some of the Israelites caused them to keep part of what they had collected until the next morning, and so it spoiled (v. 20).

The provision of manna for the people would continue throughout their forty years in the desert, and they would eat it "until they reached the border of Canaan" (v. 35). They would no longer need it when they celebrated their first Passover in the Promised Land, and therefore God would stop supplying it (Josh. 5:10-12). To serve as a reminder of His providence, an omer of manna was to be put in a jar (v. 33) made of gold (Heb. 9:4) and to be kept for future generations. Its place of deposit was to be the "Testimony" (v. 34), a title later applied to the Ark of the Covenant (25:22; 26:33). The word "Testimony" is virtually synonymous with the Ten Commandments, which are often called the "two tablets of the Testimony" (31:18; 32:15; 34:29) and which were later placed in the Ark (25:16, 21) along with the jar of manna (Heb. 9:4).

3. *The third crisis: Thirst again* (17:1-7). The people of Israel continued to travel "from place to place" (v. 1). A brief list of specific sites is given in Numbers 33:12-14, including Dophkah (probably modern Serabit el-Khadem in west central Sinai, where the Egyptians had a flourishing turquoise-mining industry). When the Israelites arrived at Rephidim (probably either Wadi Refayid or Wadi Feiran, both of which are not far from Jebel Musa, the traditional site of Mount Sinai, in the southeastern region of the peninsula) they again discovered that no drinking water was available (v. 1). That time they were guilty of putting the Lord to the test (v. 2) instead of submitting to God's testing of them, as before (15:25; 16:4).

But the Lord, as always, was equal to the occasion and graciously supplied His people's need. He told Moses that if he struck "the rock at Horeb" with the same staff with which he had earlier struck the Nile (7:20), water would flow out of the rock (v. 6). Moses obeyed the Lord's command, and water came forth to quench the thirst of the Israelites, whom Moses here referred to as "these people" (v. 4)—a note of distance and alienation often found in the prophets when they referred to their rebellious countrymen (Isa. 6:9; Hag. 1:2)

Because the people had decided to "quarrel" with Moses and to put the Lord to the "test" (v. 2), Moses named the place of the miracle both *Massah* ("Testing") and *Meribah* ("Quarreling"). Massah is referred to also in Deuteronomy 6:16; 9:22; 33:8, and both names are mentioned in Psalm 95:8. Hebrews 3:7-8, 15 quotes Psalm 95:7-8, defining Massah as "testing" and Meribah as "rebellion." Another Meribah, the site of a similar incident that occurred near Kadesh Barnea (Num. 20:1-13), is frequently referred to elsewhere (Num. 20:24; 27:14; Deut. 32:51; 33:8; Pss. 81:7; 106:32; Ezek. 47:19; 48:28). The first miracle of striking the rock and bringing forth water (see also Deut. 8:15) would later be celebrated by Israel's hymn writers and prophets (Pss. 78:15-16, 20; 105:41; 114:8; Isa. 48:21).

The Lord said to Moses in verse 6, "I will stand there before you by the rock." Paul may have had this incident in mind when he spoke of Christ as "the spiritual rock" that accompanied Israel on their journey across the desert (1 Cor. 10:4; see also Heb. 11:24-26).

4. *The fourth crisis: War* (17:8-16). The Amalekite attack on Israel at Rephidim was especially reprehensible because they "cut off all who were lagging behind" (Deut. 25:18), which would have included those who were sick, helpless, and weary. The Amalekites were a tribal group living in Sinai and southwest Canaan as early as the patriarchal period (Gen. 14:7) and were later known as "first among the nations" (Num. 24:20), possibly because they were the first people to attack the Israelites.

"Joshua" was the name given by Moses to Hoshea son of Nun (Num. 13:16). He was from the tribe of Ephraim (13:8), and his military prowess is evident from the first time we meet him (vv. 9, 13). "Hoshea" means "Salvation," whereas "Joshua" means "The LORD Is Salvation." The Greek form of the name is the same as that of the name *Jesus* (for the meaning of which see Matthew 1:21). Joshua was to become Moses' aide (Exod. 24:13; 33:11) and successor (Deut. 1:38; 3:28; 31:14; 34:9; Josh. 1:5) and would still later be the conqueror of Canaan.

Hur (v. 10; 24:14) was perhaps the same man who was the grandfather of Bezalel (1 Chron. 2:19-20), one of the builders of the Tabernacle (Exod. 31:2-5). Aaron and Hur helped Moses hold up his hands (v. 12) as a symbol of appeal to God for divine help and enablement (9:22, 29; 10:12; 14:16). As a result of the faith and courage of all those men, Israel defeated Amalek, and Moses was told to write down the story of the battle so that it would never be forgotten (v. 14).

Moses' major role in writing the first five books of the Bible is emphasized over and over (24:4; 34:27-28; Num. 33:2; Deut. 28:58; 29:20-21, 27; 30:10; 31:9, 19, 22—and especially Deut. 31:24). Scrolls of the kind used by Moses (v. 14) were long, narrow sheets of leather or papyrus on which scribes wrote with pen (Isa. 8:1) and ink (Jer. 36:18), sometimes on both sides (Ezek. 2:10; Rev. 5:1). Because they were awkward to read and difficult to store, soon after the time of Christ the scroll gave way to the book format still used today.

The fact that God ordered His people to fight their enemies on the field of battle has often caused consternation to readers of the Bible. Many have charged God with being cruel and bloodthirsty, and others have tried to dissociate the Old Testament God of wrath from the New Testament God of love. But God's love appears often in the Old Testament (in Deuteronomy and Hosea, for example) and His wrath is found often in the New (in Revelation, for example). The same holy God always loves sinners at the same time that He always hates their sins. When people persist in rebelling against Him He punishes them, and if they eventually pass the point of no return they bring about their own destruction and their doom is sealed. Willful, unrepentant, sinful conduct—like that of the pharaoh of the Exodus, for example—always brings divine judgment, whether the agent of that judgment is impersonal (such as during Noah's Flood or against Sodom and Gomorrah) or personal (such as during the conquest of Canaan).

Although God is patient and slow to anger, "abounding in love and faithfulness" (Exod. 34:6), He "does not leave the guilty unpunished" (34:7). He sometimes uses the battlefield as an arena of judgment against those who, like the Amalekites, are persistent in their refusal to fear Him (Deut. 25:18).[2]

5. *The fifth crisis: Overwork* (18:1-27). After the arrival of Moses' family (along with the other Israelites) at Rephidim, he must have sent his wife and children on ahead to Midian (vv. 2-3). Zipporah, Gershom, and Eliezer, together with Moses' father-in-law, Jethro, then joined Moses later in the desert near the mountain of God (v. 5). Jethro was especially interested in learning all about "the good things the LORD had done for Israel" (v. 9). So impressed was he by what he heard that he made a remarkable confession: "Now I know that the LORD is greater than all other gods" (v. 11; see the similar statement of Naaman the Aramean in 2 Kings 5:15). Jethro then "brought" sacrifices to God (v. 12), a verb that always means to "provide" an animal for sacrifice (25:2; Lev. 12:8, for example), never to "officiate at" a sacrifice.

Now that Moses had provided a ministry in the life of his father-in-law, it was Jethro's turn to help Moses. He asked why Moses was trying to arbitrate every dispute among the

2. For further discussion of this sensitive issue see especially Peter C. Craigie, *The Problem of War in the Old Testament* (Grand Rapids: Eerdmans, 1978); John W. Wenham, *The Goodness of God* (Downers Grove, Ill.: Inter-Varsity, 1974), pp. 99-101, 119-25, 165-68.

Israelites all by himself (v. 14). Moses responded by saying it was because the people in question came to him "to seek God's will" (v. 15), a process usually satisfied either by going to a place of worship (Gen. 25:22; Num. 27:21) or by consulting a prophet (1 Sam. 9:9; 1 Kings 22:8). Moses then informed the parties of "God's decrees and laws" (v. 16)—an indication that compiling the body of revealed law that would govern the newly formed nation of Israel had already begun (see also Exod. 15:25-26).

Jethro warned Moses that what he was doing was not good (v. 17), that he was being overworked. His advice to Moses was right on target, and he often used terminology that has a modern ring: Moses and the people who came to him would wear themselves out (v. 18), "the work [was] too heavy" for one man (v. 18), Moses should delegate responsibility on the basis of a carefully prepared administrative flow-chart (v. 21), Moses' work-load needed to be made lighter (v. 22), he needed to be willing to relinquish some of his duties and share them with others (v. 22), and the end result would be the reduction of executive strain and the increase of client satisfaction (v. 24).

Moses, even at the age of eighty (which could have seriously compounded his difficulties), had the good sense to take his father-in-law's advice (v. 24). He chose as his helpers the right kind of men—capable, God-fearing, trustworthy, honest (v. 21)—and from then on they were to decide the simpler cases, bringing only the most difficult ones to Moses. The men chosen were also to be the leading men of their tribes (Deut. 1:15), men who were "wise, understanding and respected" (1:13). And whether any individual decision was rendered by Moses himself or by one of his representatives, it was always taken for granted that "judgment belongs to God" (Deut. 1:17).

9

COVENANT

Exodus 19:1—20:17

III. Israel at Sinai: Revelation (19:1—40-38)

We have now come to the last of the three main sections of
the book of Exodus. It contains twenty-two of the forty
chapters in the book, and it is longer than the first two sections put together. Although some of it is repetitive
(35:4—38:20 and 39:1-31, for example, repeat earlier sections
of the book, sometimes almost word for word), it contains
vital teaching about God's gracious provision for the life and
worship of His redeemed people.

A. Provision for Life: The Covenant (19:1—24:18)

Our Bible is divided into two Testaments: Old and New.
The word for "testament" can also be translated
"covenant," a term that implies significant and intimate relationship between two parties (whether collective or individual). Many Scripture passages compare and contrast the
"old" or "first" covenant with the "new covenant" (see, for
example, Jer. 31:31-34; Heb. 9:15-22). Although the Bible
(particularly the Old Testament) describes many covenants in
detail, the terms *old covenant* and *first covenant* always refer
to the one we are about to study, the Mosaic (Sinaitic) covenant (see especially 2 Cor. 3:14-15; Heb. 9:15-20), the most
important of the older covenants. The Old Testament, then,
is basically the story of redemption ratified by the "old covenant" (the Mosaic covenant), and the New Testament is

basically the story of redemption ratified by the "new covenant" (instituted by Jesus during the Last Supper; see Luke 22:20). Both covenants became effective only through the shedding of blood (Exod. 24:8; Matt. 26:28).

1. *Establishment of the covenant* (19:1-25). The Israelites arrived at the Desert of Sinai exactly three months after leaving Egypt (v. 1). All the events recorded in Exodus 19:1 through Numbers 10:10 took place there, where the Israelites spent almost a year before setting out on the next stage of their journey to Canaan (Num. 10:11-12). The "mountain" (v. 2) in front of which they camped was Mount Sinai (v. 11), traditionally identified with modern *Jebel Musa* ("Mountain of Moses" in Arabic), a granite peak that rises to a height of 7,400 feet in the southeast Sinai peninsula.

As "Israel" and "Jacob" are synonyms in 1:1, so are they here as well (v. 3). The Lord reminded Moses that divine punishment had fallen on Egypt and that God Himself had carried His people "on eagles' wings" (v. 4). The female of the golden eagle (*Aquila chrysaetus*), who swoops under her fluttering young ones to catch them on her outspread wings (see especially Deut. 32:10-11), is probably the bird referred to here.

Exodus 19:5-6 (together with Gen. 12:1-3; Isa. 49:6) is often called the Old Testament equivalent of the Great Commission (also given at a mountain; see Matt. 28:16-20). The nations of the ancient Near East during the days of Moses entered into two basic types of treaties, or covenants, with each other, today referred to as parity treaties and suzerainty treaties.[1] A parity covenant would be instituted between equals, whereas a suzerainty covenant would impose terms of surrender by the king of a superior power on the ruler of an

---

1. George E. Mendenhall, "Covenant Forms in Israelite Tradition," in *The Biblical Archaeologist Reader 3,* ed. Edward F. Campbell, Jr. and David N. Freedman (Garden City, N.Y.: Doubleday, 1970), pp. 25-53.

inferior power. God's covenants with His people are always suzerainty covenants, unilaterally established by Him alone. He is the divine King, and we are His human subjects. He therefore referred to His covenant with Israel at Mount Sinai as "My" (v. 5) covenant.

Rather than interpreting God's covenant with the Israelites here as the institution of a brand new relationship, it is best to understand it as the logical outgrowth and expansion of His covenant with Abraham and his descendants six hundred years earlier (Gen. 15:9-21; 17:1-22). As participation in the divine blessings of the Abrahamic covenant was conditioned on obedience and faith (Gen. 17:1, 9; 18:19; 22:18; 26:4-5; Deut. 30:15-20), so also the Sinaitic covenant was conditional: "If you obey me fully and keep my covenant, then out of all nations you will be my treasured possession" (v. 5). The implication is clear: Disobedience would bring curses (Deut. 28:15-68) instead of blessings (28:1-14)—and the section on curses in Deuteronomy 28 is four times as long as the section on blessings.

The four phrases "out of all nations," "treasured possession," "kingdom of priests," and "holy nation" (vv. 5-6) find their respective parallels in 1 Peter 2:9, where they are used of Christians: "chosen people," "people belonging to God," "royal priesthood," "holy nation." God has called us "out of darkness into his wonderful light" (1 Pet. 2:9), just as He did the Israelites at the time of the Exodus. The term "treasured possession" (Deut. 7:6; 14:2; 26:18; Ps. 135:4; Mal. 3:17) refers to a prized item such as a precious heirloom that its owner delights in and carefully preserves. "Although the whole earth" (v. 5) and everything in it was created by God and belongs to Him (Gen. 14:19, 22; Ps. 24:1-2), Israel is His special treasure. The ancient equivalents of church and state were not separated from each other, as the phrases "kingdom of priests" and "holy nation" demonstrate ("kingdom" and "nation," although "state" words, are combined with "priests" and "holy," which are "church" words). Every believer is to engage in priestly, intercessory, reconciling ministry (Isa. 61:6; 1 Pet. 2:5; Rev. 1:6; 5:10; 20:6), and God's people individually and collectively are to be holy—that is, set apart to do His will (Deut. 7:6; 14:2, 21; 26:19; Isa. 62:12).

Although the specific terms of the covenant had not yet been spelled out to them, the Israelites at Sinai agreed to obey them (v. 8) and renewed their intention to do so even after they heard the full list of stipulations (24:3, 7; Deut. 5:27). Unfortunately, they and their descendants would break those early pledges repeatedly (see, for example, Jer. 31:32; Hos. 4:1-2; 8:12; 9:17; 11:2; Amos 2:4), ultimately making the new covenant necessary.

The "dense cloud" (v. 9) in which the Lord descended to the top of Mount Sinai was probably not the pillar of cloud mentioned earlier (13:21). The former was associated with "thunder and lightning," "a very loud trumpet blast" (v. 16), "smoke" and "fire" (v. 18)—not an indication of a volcanic eruption but an astounding cosmic display of the kind that often accompanies God's arrival (2 Thess. 1:7; Heb. 12:18-19; Rev. 4:1, 5; 11:19). The Israelites heard God's voice speaking to them (v. 9) out of the fire, but they saw no form of any kind (Deut. 4:15) because God is spirit (Isa. 31:3; John 4:24).

To properly worship such a God requires both outward and inward preparation (vv. 10-15). Just as Moses was earlier commanded to remove his sandals on the "holy ground" where God met him (3:5), so now the people were to keep their distance from the holy mountain (vv. 12-13, 23; Heb. 12:20). They were also to "abstain from sexual relations" (v. 15), not because such activity was inherently sinful but because it might leave the participants ceremonially unclean (Lev. 15:18). The sights and sounds on the mountain terrified the people (v. 16), and Moses trembled with fear as well (Heb. 12:21; see also Deut. 9:19). "A smoking fire pot with a blazing torch" (Gen. 15:17) symbolized the presence of God at the institution of the Abrahamic covenant, and in a similar way "fire" along with "smoke" as though "from a furnace" (v. 18) accompanied the appearance of God on Mount Sinai at the time of the institution of the Mosaic covenant. The "priests" (vv. 22, 24) on the scene at the foot of the mountain were either elders (3:18; 12:21; 18:12) or younger men (24:5), the two groups authorized to perform priestly functions until the establishment of Aaron's priesthood (28:1).

2. *Statement of the covenant* (20:1-17). Probably only because of archaeological "accident," the best examples of ancient Near Eastern suzerainty treaties have been preserved in archives from the end of the Hittite empire (about 1450-1200 B.C.). The formal literary structure of the first three sections of the typical Hittite suzerainty covenant of this period, which is contemporary with the time of Moses, sheds light on the significance of Exodus 20:1-17 and Deuteronomy 5:1-3, 6-22.

The first section, called the preamble, contains the self-identification of the suzerain: "Thus say So-and-So, the great king, the king of the land of the Hittites, the son of Such-and-Such." It usually then adds other titles and attributes of the ruler. The second section, known as the historical prologue, details the positive relationships that have existed between the suzerain and his new vassal up to the time of the treaty. The third section, usually the longest of all, is known as the stipulations section and consists of the bill of particulars to which the vassal is expected to submit. The rationale behind that arrangement of sections is probably as follows: On the basis of the first section (telling who the suzerain is) and the second section (listing the good things he has done for the vassal in the past), the third section sets forth the duties and obligations now to be imposed on the vassal.

Introduction (20:1). The Hittites referred to the treaty "stipulations" (the third section) as the "words" (see v. 1; 24:3, 8; 34:28). The stipulations of the Mosaic covenant are found in 20:3-17, known more familiarly as the Ten Commandments (34:28; Deut. 4:13; 10:4), the Hebrew words which mean literally "Ten Words." "Decalogue," a term of Greek origin sometimes used as a synonym for the Ten Commandments, also means literally "Ten Words." The term "words'" in verse 1, therefore, probably applies only to verses 3-17 and does not include verse 2.

Preamble and Historical Prologue (20:2). The statement "I am the LORD your God," brief and to the point, is the majestic preamble of the Mosaic covenant. The phrase "who brought you out of Egypt, out of the land of slavery," almost as brief as the preamble, is a condensed summary of God's mighty acts in the past and serves as the historical prologue for what follows.

Stipulations (20:3-17). The Ten Commandments flow naturally from what God has said in essence in verse 2: "On the basis of who I am, and on the basis of what I have done for you, here now is what you are to do for Me."

The first commandment: God's being (20:3). In the light of our new understanding of the Ten Commandments in the context of ancient treaties, scholars who have claimed verse 2 to be the first commandment can no longer make a valid case because it is now clear that it constitutes the preamble and historical prologue of the Mosaic covenant. In any event, verse 2 is a statement of fact rather than a commandment demanding compliance.

If "before" is the right translation in verse 3, the first commandment means, "You shall have no other gods in preference to me," whereas if "besides" is correct, the commandment means, "You shall have no other gods in addition to me." Perhaps better than either translation would be this rendering: "You shall have no other gods whatever, because all of them oppose me." The Hebrew for the word "before" in verse 3 is translated "in hostility toward" in Genesis 16:12; 25:18. The first commandment teaches, then, that no deity, real or imagined, is to rival the one true God, who is the only one that matters.

The second commandment: God's worship (20:4-6). It

would make good sense to combine the second commandment with the first and then call verses 3-6 together one commandment. Those who do so, however, must either call it the
second commandment and call verse 2 the first commandment (which unfortunately cannot be done because, as we saw
above, verse 2 is the preamble and historical prologue), or
they must call verses 3-6 the first commandment and then
split the tenth commandment into two, making it the ninth
and tenth commandments, as follows: "You shall not covet
your neighbor's house" (ninth); "You shall not covet your
neighbor's wife" (tenth). But that arrangement will not work
either, since Deuteronomy 5:21 transposes "house" and
"wife" (which means that the ninth commandment in Exodus
would become the tenth in Deuteronomy and the tenth in Exodus would be the ninth in Deuteronomy). All things considered, then, it would seem best to adhere to the traditional
enumeration as proposed by Palestinian Jews such as Philo
and Josephus, by church Fathers such as Origen, by the
Eastern Orthodox church, and by the Reformed churches.

The second commandment teaches that since God has no
visible form, any idol intended to resemble Him would be a
sinful misrepresentation of Him (Deut. 4:12, 15-18). No other
Gods are to be worshiped (v. 5); therefore making idols of
them would be equally sinful (Deut. 4:19, 23-28). The people
of other nations might worship objects "in heaven above"
(such as the sun, moon, and stars) or "on the earth beneath"
(such as land animals) or "in the waters below" (such as
crocodiles in Egypt or sea monsters among the Babylonians),
but Israel was to worship only the one true God. He is
"jealous" (v. 5)—that is, zealous (not envious or suspicious)
to vindicate His people (Isa. 9:7) and to deliver to judgment
all who oppose Him (Deut. 29:20). His zeal also demands ex-
clusive devotion to Himself (Exod. 34:14; Deut. 4:24; 32:16,
21; Josh. 24:19; Ps. 78:58; 1 Cor. 10:22). "Thousands" (v. 6)
means "a thousand generations," forming a contrast to "the
third and fourth generation" of verse 5 (see also Deut. 7:9;

1 Chron. 16:15; Ps. 105:8). Keeping God's commandments flows naturally from loving Him (v. 6; John 14:15; 1 John 5:3).

The third commandment: God's name (20:7). To "misuse" the name of the Lord is to profane God and His name by using it when taking a false oath (Lev. 19:12; see also Jer. 7:9), as on the witness stand in court. In His Sermon on the Mount, Jesus elaborated on the subject of oath-taking (Matt. 5:33-37). Profanation of God's name has become frighteningly common in modern times, and yet it is among the most serious of all sins. To degrade His name is to degrade Him, and "he will not hold anyone guiltless" who does so.

The fourth commandment: God's day (20:8-11). "Six days" (v. 9) is the maximum work week, not the minimum. The commandment has nothing to do with the question of a short work week. Three reasons are given for not doing "any work" (v. 10) on the Sabbath day: After creation God "rested on the seventh day" (v. 11), and therefore so must the Israelites; because the Israelites rested, so must their servants (Deut. 5:14); Sabbath rest is in contrast to Egyptian slavery, from which God redeemed the Israelites (Deut. 5:15). The Sabbath would therefore become the "sign" of the Mosaic covenant (Exod. 31:12-17), just as the rainbow was the sign of the Noahic covenant (Gen. 9:12-13) and circumcision the sign of the Abrahamic covenant (17:11).

The fifth commandment: God's representatives (20:12). "Honor your father and your mother" concludes a group of commandments concerning our responsibilities toward God and begins a group concerning our responsibilities toward our fellowmen. It therefore serves as a transitional commandment between the two groups. But since eight of the commandments (numbers one through three and six through ten) are expressed negatively, it is perhaps best to view the fourth commandment (which is expressed in positive terms) as concluding the first group and the fifth commandment (also expressed positively) as beginning—and being a part of—the second group. Its contents also fit the second group better than the first.

To "honor" means to prize highly (Prov. 4:8), to care for (Ps. 9:15), to show respect for (Lev. 19:3), and to obey (but only "in the Lord," Eph. 6:1). The fifth commandment is "the first commandment with a promise" (Eph. 6:2-3).

The sixth commandment: Man's life (20:13). The Hebrew word for "murder" always stresses premeditation and deliberateness. It applies to accomplices as well as to actual murderers (1 Kings 21:19). In Jesus' eyes, anger and contempt are tantamount to murder (Matt. 5:21-22).

The seventh commandment: Man's family (20:14). Adultery is a sin "against God" (Gen. 39:9) as well as against the offended marriage partner. Jesus teaches that lust is equivalent to the act of adultery (Matt. 5:27-28).

The eighth commandment: Man's property (20:15). Holding back a worker's wages (Lev. 19:13), engaging in dishonest business practices (19:35), charging exorbitant rates of interest (25:36)—all are subtle forms of theft that steal not only from man but also from God, the ultimate Owner of everything (25:23).

The ninth commandment: Man's reputation (20:16). Lying (falsehood in speech) and stealing (falsehood in action) are equally deceptive (Lev. 19:11). Human depravity insures that "false testimony" would be universally practiced (because it is difficult to detect), and so a plurality of witnesses is required in court cases (Deut. 17:6-7; 19:15-19).

The tenth commandment: Man's security (20:17). To "covet" is to desire with evil motivation anything that is not one's own. "Evil thoughts" often head the list of overt and visible sins (Matt. 15:19), and to break God's commandments inwardly is equivalent to breaking them outwardly (Matt. 5:21-30). David's coveting of Bathsheba resulted in adultery and murder.

Jesus summarized the Ten Commandments by condensing them into two. He said that "the first and greatest commandment" is this: "Love the Lord your God with all your heart and with all your soul and with all your mind" (Matt. 22:37, quoting Deut. 6:5). He then went on to say that "the second is like it: 'Love your neighbor as yourself' " (Matt. 22:38, quoting Lev. 19:18). He concluded by boldly claiming that "all the Law and the Prophets hang on these two commandments" (Matt 22:40). Jesus was saying essentially that love for God (that is, obeying the first four of the Ten Commandments) and love for neighbor (that is, obeying the last six of the Ten Commandments) constitute the basic teaching of the Old Testament.

Jesus understood love, the most positive force in the universe, as the total intent and thrust of the Ten Commandments. Psychiatrist Karl Menninger says much the same thing in his definition of love as "the medicine for the sickness of the world." The blend of ingredients in God's prescription for human happiness known as the Ten Commandments is guaranteed, if taken, to keep us spiritually strong and healthy. To obey His covenant stipulations is to receive His bountiful blessings.

10

LAW

Exodus 20:18—24:18

Law—and order—are absolutely basic to human society. Perhaps that is why the earliest and most numerous of all ancient writings (about 3500-3400 B.C.) are legal texts that guarantee individual rights as well as harmony within the community.[1] Because human nature is sinful, laws to regulate human relationships are essential.

Under ordinary circumstances, however, governments do not give awards to people who obey the laws of the land. It is simply expected that every person will be a law-abiding citizen. Only when laws are violated does it become necessary for governmental officials to intervene—not to reward, but to punish.

Is that why so many people tend to fear or even despise law, whether civil or spiritual? That would seem to be the case. Since God's law is holy (Rom. 7:12), no one has ever kept it perfectly (Gal. 3:10). All have sinned and fallen short of the glory of God (Rom. 3:23), and all attempts to gain salvation by obeying the law are futile and doomed to failure. Three times in one verse (Gal. 2:16) Paul tells us that no one can be justified by observing the law—and that was just as true for Old Testament believers as it is for New Testament believers. The ancient Israelite, like the modern Christian, obeyed the law not in order to be redeemed but because he had already been redeemed. The exodus through the Sea of Reeds preceded the lawgiving atop Mount Sinai.

---

1. See D. J. Wiseman, "Law and Order in Old Testament Times," *Vox Evangelica* 7 (1973): 7.

The Ten Commandments, then, far from being a negative set of statutes to make God's people miserable, were a gracious gift from the Lord to insure the kind of community that would keep the Israelites healthy and happy. But the Decalogue itself is quite brief and could therefore not be expected to cover all the ceremonial and legal questions that would arise. Explanations of and expansions on the basic stipulations of the Ten Commandments would soon become necessary, and God—as always—was ready to meet that need.

3. *Expansion of the covenant* (20:18—23:33). The section before us has something to say about each of the Ten Commandments, even if only incidentally. Exodus 20:23 and 22:20 refer to the being and worship of God (commandments one and two), whereas 22:11 relates to the third commandment. Sabbath laws pertinent to the fourth commandment are outlined in 23:10-13. The death penalty is invoked upon those who attack or curse their parents (21:15, 17) in violation of the fifth commandment. The distinction between deliberate murder (see the sixth commandment) and unintentional manslaughter is affirmed in 21:12-14. Since the sin of adultery (commandment seven) is self-explanatory, nothing further needs to be said about it, but other sexual sins are condemned in 22:16-17, 19. Various kinds of theft (commandment eight) receive extended treatment in 21:16 and 22:1-15, and the ramifications of giving false testimony (see the ninth commandment) are described in 23:1-9. Coveting (commandment ten), which deals with motivation and therefore relates to all of our voluntary actions, is present in one form or other throughout this entire section (see, for example, 21:13-14).

Exodus 20:18—23:33, known as the "Book of the Covenant" (24:7), is probably Israel's oldest law code. Other ancient law codes in the Near East, however, including the Sumerian formulations of Urnammu and Lipit-Ishtar as well as the Babylonian codes of Eshnunna and Hammurapi, preceded the Book of the Covenant by several centuries.

Their similarities to Israel's legislation are impressive but understandable, since all ancient Near Eastern law arose in the same basic cultural context. But the Book of the Covenant, inspired by the Lord through Moses, differs markedly from non-Israelite law codes in its concern for the widow, the orphan, the poor, the defenseless, all of whom receive special attention and providential care from God Himself (see, for example, 21:26-27; 22:21-27; 23:6-9). Such evenhanded and humane treatment of people who find themselves in difficult circumstances is almost never a part of ancient law codes outside the Bible.

The Book of the Covenant follows the practice of certain other ancient legal documents by opening with a prologue and closing with an epilogue.

Book of the Covenant: Prologue (20:18-21). After the Lord's solemn declaration of the Ten Commandments, Exodus 20:18-21 summarizes the awesome scene at the holy mountain (19:16-25) to serve as an introduction to the expansion of the Decalogue in the Book of the Covenant. Although the people "trembled with fear" (v. 18), Moses said to them, "Do not be afraid" (v. 20)—that is, "Do not be filled with alarm and horror." Instead, they were to experience the "fear of God" (v. 20) in the sense of bowing down before Him in reverence and awe. Their frightened plea to Moses that he should ask God not to speak to them (v. 19) is referred to in Hebrews 12:19, where a contrast is drawn between the limited access to God that the people had at Mount Sinai under the old covenant and the complete fellowship with God that we have at "Mount Zion" (Heb. 12:22) under the "new covenant" (12:24) through the Lord Jesus.

Book of the Covenant: Body (20:22—23:19). Although some commentators have claimed to find exactly seventy laws in this section (seventy being the ideal and complete number of Jacob's descendants who originally went down into

Egypt), all such attempts have proved to be more ingenious than convincing. In any event, the individual laws here and elsewhere in the Mosaic legislation are of two kinds: casuistic or conditional ("If/Whoever/Anyone who . . .") and apodictic or categorical ("Do/Do not . . ."; "You shall/You shall not . . ."). The former is typical case law and is attested universally in ancient Near Eastern law codes, whereas the latter is almost never found outside the Old Testament and represents the unique contribution of the people of Israel as mediated to them by divine command.

Proper worship is the subject of 20:22-26. The Lord had descended "from heaven" (v. 22)—His permanent dwelling place—to "the top of Mount Sinai" (19:20) in order to tell the Israelites not to make or worship idols (v. 23), which are powerless to help their worshipers (Pss. 115:4-7; 135:5-6, 15-17). Israelite altars were made of earth (v. 24), unworked stones (v. 25), or wood (27:1). An altar of earth, with dimensions the same as those of the Tabernacle courtyard altar (27:1), has been found in the excavated ruins of a small temple from the Solomonic period at Arad in southern Israel. The purpose of "burnt offerings" (v. 24) was to atone for sin, whereas the "fellowship offerings" gave the people an opportunity to enjoy communion with the Lord.

Altars built with "dressed stones" (v. 25) were forbidden to the Israelites (Deut. 27:5-6; Josh. 8:30-31), although such altars were routinely made by pagans and have been found in ancient sites throughout Palestine. Many altars of this type have "steps" (v. 26) alongside them, prohibited in early Israel because scantily clad priests who ascended them would expose their nakedness to onlookers (the oldest altar in Palestine is stepped and was excavated in an Early Bronze Age stratum at Megiddo). Later, when God allowed His people to build stepped altars (Lev. 9:22; Ezek. 43:17), Aaron and his descendants had already been instructed to wear linen underclothes (Exod. 28:42-43; Lev. 6:10; 16:3-4; Ezek. 44:17-18).

Exodus 21:1-11 regulates the sale and treatment of servants

(see also Lev. 25:39-55; Deut. 15:12-18; Jer. 34:8-22). We cannot be sure whether "Hebrew" here is a synonym for "Israelite" or whether it refers to a member of the non-Israelite 'apiru population (see commentary at 1:15). In any case, the purchased servant was to be freed after six years of work (v. 2), just as the cultivated land was to have a sabbath year of rest (Lev. 25:2-5). The word "love" (v. 5) is used in a legal sense here, although overtones of loyalty and affection for a generous and kind master should not be entirely ruled out. The term "judges" (v. 6; see also 22:8-9, 28) translates the Hebrew word *elohim* (usually rendered "God" or "gods") and reflects the practice of requiring a plaintiff or defendant to appear in court and take an oath in the name of God (or "the gods," if the context was pagan). Piercing a servant's ear with "an awl" (v. 6; Deut. 15:17) symbolized submission to willing obedience (Ps. 40:2-8). Verses 7-11 indicate the generally inferior status of maidservants, although even here the treatment of them is far more humane than among non-Israelite peoples.

Verses 12-17 describe sins and crimes that demand the exaction of the death penalty (for further details see Deut. 21:1-9; 24:7; 27:24-25). Verse 12 expands on 20:13 and sanctions capital punishment (see also Gen. 9:6), but only for deliberate and premeditated murder. If unintentional manslaughter (v. 13; for related expressions see Num. 35:11, 22-23; Deut. 19:4) was committed and "God [let] it happen" (v. 13—that is, the occurrence was an "act of God," beyond human control), the perpetrator had the right to "flee to a place" (v. 13) of worship in a city of refuge (Num. 35:6-32; Deut. 19:1-13; Josh. 20:1-9; 21:13, 21, 27, 32, 38). But taking hold of the horns of the altar there (v. 14) provided immunity from punishment only if the fugitive had killed someone accidentally (see 1 Kings 1:50-51; 2:28).

Laws concerning personal injury are outlined in verses 18-27. If an injured man "[walked] around outside with his staff" (v. 19), he was obviously convalescing in a satisfactory way, but the one who caused the injury must compensate him for "the loss of his time"—that is, his enforced idleness (literally "his sitting"; v. 19). Verses 20-21 indicate that a slaveholder should be given the benefit of the doubt when maltreatment of his slaves resulted in their death but no homicidal intentions could be proved.

The complexities involved in attempting to interpret verse 22 make it unwise to press it into service in the abortion controversy, pro or con. Other passages (for example, Amos 1:13-14; 2 Kings 15:16), however, make clear that unfeeling destruction of unborn fetuses is sinful and calls forth divine judgment. The "serious injury" (vv. 22-23) pertains to both mother and child, and the "life for life" of verse 23 is an exception to the regulation of verse 13 due to the gravity of the crime here described.

Verses 26-27 give two examples of humane application of the so-called "law of retaliation," the famous "eye for eye, tooth for tooth" principle (vv. 24-25; Lev. 24:19-20; Deut. 19:21). The divine intent of the law was to limit the punishment to fit the crime, not to provide opportunity for vengeance. When Jesus invoked the law of love (Matt. 5:38-42), He corrected any possible misunderstanding of the law of retaliation.

Injuries caused by or inflicted on animals are treated in verses 28-36. The goring bull that caused death or injury (vv. 28-32, 35-36) was such a serious problem in ancient times that most of the major nonbiblical law codes also contained regulations dealing with it. A bull that killed someone became accountable for that person's life (v. 28; see Gen. 9:5). The owner of a habitually goring bull that killed someone was also subject to the death penalty (v. 29), but he could redeem his own life by making whatever "payment" (v. 30; literally "ransom," as in Num. 35:31) was demanded. If a slave was gored, the bull's owner had to pay to the master of the slave "thirty shekels of silver" (v. 32). Apparently the standard price for a slave, it was the amount Judas was willing to accept as his fee for betraying Jesus (Matt. 26:14-15; see also Zech. 11:12-13). The shekel weighed about two-fifths of an ounce and was not a coin in Moses' time, since coinage was invented in the seventh century B.C.

Exodus 22:1-15 is composed of laws regulating property rights (see 20:15). Restitution for a stolen ox was more costly than for a stolen sheep (v. 1) because a trained ox was more valuable than a sheep. An act of self-defense against a thief who broke in at night (see Job 24:16) did not produce blood-guilt even if the thief died (v. 2), but killing an intruder in broad daylight was not justifiable (v. 3). Restitution for destroyed property must be made from "the best" (v. 5) of the guilty party's own resources, emphasizing the importance of quality and generosity. A fire that spread into "thorn-bushes" (v. 6) endangered neighboring property, since thorn-bushes were often used as hedges (Mic. 7:4) between cultivated fields. Laws similar to those in verses 10-13 were apparently in force as early as the patriarchal period (see Gen. 31:39).

Verses 16-31 constitute a series of general laws concerning social obligations and expectations. The "bride-price" (vv. 16-17) was a gift, often substantial (see Deut. 22:28-29), given by a prospective groom to the bride's family as payment for her (see Gen. 24:53), a custom still followed in the Middle East. Sorcery (v. 18) was only one of a number of occult practices forbidden to Israel (see Deut. 18:10, 14; 1 Sam. 28:9; Isa. 47:12-14). Bestiality (v. 19; see also Lev. 18:23; 20:15-16; Deut. 27:21), although prohibited among the Israelites, was practiced by pagan gods and demigods in Babylon and Canaan, as their own religious epics indicate. Idolatry (see Exod. 20:3-5) was such an abomination to the Lord that anyone (whether Israelite or Canaanite) who practiced it was to be totally "destroyed" (v. 20; Num. 21:2; Deut. 2:34; 3:6; 7:2; 13:15; 20:17; Josh. 2:10; 6:17, 21; 8:25; 10:1, 28, 35, 37, 39-40; 11:11-12, 20-21; Judg. 1:17).

The "alien" (v. 21), the "widow," the "orphan" (v. 22),

the "needy" (v. 25)—were all objects of God's providential care and compassion (v. 27; 23:6-12; Lev. 19:9-10; Deut. 14:29; 16:11, 14; 24:19-21; 26:12-13; Pss. 10:14, 17-18; 68:5; 82:3; 146:9; Isa. 1:23; 10:2; Jer. 7:6; 22:3; Zech. 7:10; Mal. 3:5; Matt. 25:34-45). "Interest" (v. 25) for profit was not to be charged at the expense of the poor (Lev. 25:35-37; Deut. 15:7-11; 23:19; Neh. 5:7-12; Job 24:9; Prov. 28:8; Ezek. 18:13; 22:12), and generosity in such matters was extended even further by Jesus (Luke 6:34-35). Deuteronomy 24:10-13 demands courtesy on the part of a creditor who takes another person's garment "as a pledge" (v. 26), whereas Amos 2:8 deplores the desecration of such garments.

The last part of verse 28 was quoted by Paul in repentance after he had unwittingly insulted the high priest (Acts 23:4-5). The presentation of firstborn animals to the Lord on "the eighth day" (v. 30; Lev. 22:27) is perhaps an extension of the requirement that male infants were to be circumcised when they were eight days old (Gen. 17:12). Eating the meat of an animal torn by wild beasts was forbidden to people (v. 31) and priests (Lev. 22:8) alike.

Most of the commands in 23:1-9 are expansions of 20:16. Violations of the basic principles outlined in verse 1 are recorded in Deuteronomy 22:13-19 and 1 Kings 21:9-13. Israel was to show the same kindness to enemies as to brothers (vv. 4-5; see Deut. 22:1-4; Prov. 25:21), and Jesus advanced the relationship to the highest level by invoking the law of love for one's enemies (Matt. 5:44). Deuteronomy 16:19 is an almost verbatim parallel to verse 8, which is illustrated positively by Samuel (1 Sam. 12:3) and negatively by his sons (1 Sam. 8:3).

Verses 10-13 are extensions of the Sabbath teachings of 20:8-11; Deuteronomy 5:12-15, whereas verses 14-19 concern the three annual festivals (Unleavened Bread, Harvest, and Ingathering) and are paralleled in 34:18-26 (see also Lev. 23:4-44; Num. 28:16—29:40; Deut. 16:1-17).

The "Feast of Unleavened Bread" (v. 15; 12:17-20) was

observed from the fifteenth through the twenty-first days of
Abib, the first month (mid-March to mid-April), and took
place immediately after Passover (the fourteenth day).
Celebrated at the beginning of the barley harvest, it commemorated the exodus from Egypt.

The "Feast of Harvest" (v. 16) was also called the "Feast
of Weeks" (34:22), because it was held seven weeks after the
Feast of Unleavened Bread. It was observed on the sixth day
of Sivan, the third month (mid-May to mid-June), during the
wheat harvest and commemorated the giving of the law on
Mount Sinai. It was later called the "day of Pentecost" (Acts
2:1; 20:16; 1 Cor. 16:8), a Greek word meaning "fifty" (see
Lev. 23:16).

The "Feast of Ingathering" (v. 16) was also called the
"Feast of Tabernacles" (Lev. 23:34), because the Israelites
lived in "booths" (Lev. 23:42-43) when God brought them
out of Egypt. Observed from the fifteenth through the
twenty-second days of Tishri, the seventh month (mid-
September to mid-October), when the produce of the vines
and orchards had been harvested, it commemorated the
desert wanderings after the Exodus and the giving of the law.
When dated with reference to the civil or agricultural calendar, which began in the fall, it took place "at the end of the
year" (v. 16). The prohibition against cooking "a young goat
in its mother's milk" (v. 19; 34:26; Deut. 14:21) may be a pro-
test against a pagan ritual (see also Exod. 23:33; 34:15) mentioned in a Canaanite religious text of the fifteenth century
B.C.

Book of the Covenant: Epilogue (23:20-33). An "angel"
(v. 20), together with the fire and cloud (14:19), would lead
the Israelites throughout their journey (40:36-38; Num.
9:15-23) to the land of Canaan, the "place" (v. 20) the Lord
had prepared for them. His "Name" (v. 21)—that is, His
presence (see 3:12-14)—would therefore be with them always,
and they were not to worship other gods (vv. 24-25, 32),

which would lead to their destruction (symbolized by the word "snare," v. 33; see 10:7; Job 18:9; Ps. 18:5; Prov. 13:14; 21:6; Isa. 24:17-18). To prepare the way for the invasion of Canaan, the Lord would send the "hornet" (v. 28; Deut. 7:20; Josh. 24:12), probably symbolizing Egypt's military strength (compare the symbolic use of "flies" and "bees" in Isa. 7:18). "Little by little" (v. 30; see especially Judg. 1:1-36) the land would be conquered by Israel with God's indispensable help. The "borders" (v. 31; Gen. 15:18; 1 Kings 4:21) of their new home would extend from the "Red Sea" (here referring to the Gulf of Aqaba, as in 1 Kings 9:26) on the east to the "Sea of the Philistines" (the Mediterranean) on the west and from the "desert" (in northeast Sinai) on the south to the "River" (the Euphrates; see Gen. 15:18) on the north. An exciting prospect indeed awaited the people if they would agree to remain faithful to the Lord (vv. 22, 25-26, 33).

4. *Ratification of the covenant* (24:1-18). "Nadab and Abihu" (v. 1), Aaron's two oldest sons (6:23), were among the "leaders of the Israelites" (v. 11) who had a vision of God. They later disobeyed the Lord and died as a result of their sin (Lev. 10:1-2). The elders who shared in Moses' covenant ratification ceremony numbered seventy (v. 1), corresponding to the ideal and complete number of Jacob's descendants, who had migrated to Egypt centuries earlier (1:5). Twelve stone pillars were set up "representing the twelve tribes" (v. 4) that constituted the newly formed covenant nation. The people had already agreed to do everything the Lord had said (19:8); they repeated their intention to do so (v. 3) after Moses told them all the Lord's "words" (the Ten Commandments, 20:2-17) and "laws" (the Book of the Covenant, 20:22—23:19).

Before Aaron's priesthood was established (28:1), priestly functions (including the offering of sacrifices) were performed at least partly by specially designated young men

(v. 5). In the scene before us, Moses first sprinkled half the sacrificial blood on the altar (v. 6) in recognition of the fact that God, the divine Suzerain, initiated the covenant ratification ceremony. Then Moses read aloud the Book of the Covenant (the provisions of which would continue to make an impact on God's people centuries later; see 2 Kings 23:2-3). Only after the Israelites agreed once again to obey the Lord (v. 7) did Moses sprinkle the other half of the sacrificial blood on them, symbolizing their commitment to the covenant in all its details (v. 8). The procedure described here is a modified form of other covenant ratification ceremonies portrayed in the Bible (Gen. 15:9-18; Jer. 34:18-20) and elsewhere (especially in documents from Mari on the Euphrates). In all such ceremonies the oath of obedience implied the participants' willingness to suffer the fate of the sacrificed animals if the covenant stipulations were violated by those who took the oath.

In comparing the new covenant mediated through Christ with the old covenant mediated through Moses, Hebrews 9:20 quotes part of Exodus 24:8. When Jesus instituted the Lord's Supper He said to His disciples, "This cup is the new covenant in my blood" (Luke 22:20; 1 Cor. 11:25). In so doing He reminded them—and us—that no covenant could be ratified without a blood sacrifice (see Heb. 9:18), leading to the eternal principle that "without the shedding of blood there is no forgiveness" of sin (Heb. 9:22).

A fellowship meal concluded the ratification ceremony (v. 11; see also Gen. 31:43-54). The solemnity of the occasion is underlined by the fact that although the participants saw God, He did not strike them dead. It may well be that only His feet were seen by them (v. 10). Sapphire or lapis lazuli is associated with a divine visitation also in Ezekiel 1:26, perhaps because of its sky-blue color (v. 10). To the Israelites the glory of the Lord looked like a "consuming fire" (v. 17; see also Deut. 4:24; 9:3; Heb. 12:29) on top of Mount Sinai.

There Moses stayed "forty days and forty nights" (v. 18) to receive further instructions from the God who had led him and his people to that important crossroads in their lives.

11

TABERNACLE

EXODUS 25:1—27:21; 30:1—31:18; 35:1—38:31

B. PROVISION FOR WORSHIP: THE TABERNACLE (25:1—40:38)

The final sixteen chapters of Exodus focus for the most part on the instructions for and fashioning of the Tabernacle, its furnishings, and the garments of the priests who served in it. The amount of space devoted to those topics amply demonstrates their importance to Israel's experience as a religious community. Our purpose in this chapter will be to concentrate on the Tabernacle itself together with its furnishings. We will deviate somewhat from the outline given at the end of chapter 1 in order to bring together in one place all the Exodus material related to the Tabernacle and its furnishings and to arrange that material in ways that we hope will prove helpful and instructive.

1. *The Tabernacle: Its Origin, Furnishings, and Meaning* (25:1—27:21; 30:1—31:18; 35:1—38:31).

Preparation (25:1-9; 31:1-18; 35:1—36:7; 38:21-31). Before the Tabernacle could be fashioned and furnished, the covenant embodied in it had to be given a sign, the materials for its construction had to be gathered, and the craftsmen to build it had to be appointed.

•The sign of the covenant: The Sabbath (31:12-18; 35:1-3)

As the sign of the Noahic covenant is the rainbow (Gen. 9:13), and as the sign of the Abrahamic covenant is circumcision (Gen. 17:11), the sign of the Mosaic covenant is the observation and celebration of the Sabbath day (Exod. 31:13, 17). At the end of Exodus 31, the chapter that concludes the instructions for fashioning the Tabernacle and its furnishings, the Lord reminds His people that they are not to work on the Sabbath (31:12-17) and then gives Moses the "two tablets of the Testimony" (v. 18), the tablets containing the Ten Commandments, the longest of which requires that the Sabbath be a day of rest (20:8-11).

In the first paragraph of Exodus 35, the chapter that begins the account of how the Tabernacle was actually fashioned and furnished, Moses reaffirms God's insistence that no work is to be done on the Sabbath—not even the lighting of a fire (35:1-3; to this day, orthodox Jews in some communities retain the services of Gentiles to light cooking or heating fires for them on the Sabbath). The Sabbath passages in Exodus 31 and 35 are obviously meant to warn Israel not to work on the construction of the Tabernacle or its furnishings on the Sabbath day.

•Offerings of materials for the Tabernacle (25:1-9; 30:11-16; 35:4-29; 38:21-31)

Only voluntary gifts were acceptable as materials for the Lord's house (25:2; 35:5, 21-22, 29), since love rather than compulsion is the basis of all truly biblical giving (2 Cor. 9:7). "Men and women alike" (Exod. 35:22) participated in the offerings for the Tabernacle as well as in its construction (vv. 25-26, 29). The finest materials were brought, and the most highly skilled people were chosen to perform the most intricate of tasks. God's house deserves His people's best efforts.

As to the materials themselves, the "blue, purple and scarlet yarn" (25:4) was probably three shades of dyed linen, while the "fine linen" (v. 4) was either white or undyed. "Goat hair" (v. 4) is still the primary material in Bedouin tents today. "Hides of sea cows" (v. 5) were used for the outer covering of the Tabernacle (26:14; Num. 4:25), probably because of their waterproofing qualities. The sea cow (*Dugong dugong*) is an herbivorous mammal native to the Red Sea and the Gulf of Aqaba, and to this day the Bedouin make sandals from its skin (see Ezek. 16:10, where the word for "leather" is the same as that for "sea cow" in Exodus). "Acacia" (Exod. 25:5), a member of the mimosa family, abounds, in several species from the Sinai peninsula northeastward to the Dead Sea valley as far north as Jericho. A hardy wood, it is very useful for building purposes.

Of the quantities of metals brought (38:21-31), the amount of silver is of particular interest. Since one talent equals three thousand shekels, the total amount of silver weighed 301,775 shekels (v. 25)—exactly half a shekel (see also 30:11-16) for each of the 603,550 men of military age (v. 26), no matter what his financial status (30:15). This fact strengthens the literal interpretation of the 603,550 figure as discussed earlier (see chapter 7). Gold, an especially precious metal, was presented to the Lord as a "wave offering" (35:22; 38:24; see also 38:29), a procedure that apparently involved waving the gift back and forth as it was brought before the Lord (see 29:24, 26).

The Exodus passages that discuss the materials for the Tabernacle refer to the structure itself by several different names, each of which symbolizes a particular function or purpose that it served. The best known and most common term is "tabernacle" (25:9), which means literally "dwelling place" and signifies the Lord's desire and intention to "dwell among" His people (29:45-46). Just as they lived in tents, so God also would condescend to "dwell" in a tent.

A second name for the Tabernacle that stresses the immanence—the nearness—of God is "Tent of Meeting" (35:21). The Lord desired not only to "meet" Moses and speak to him there (29:42) but also to "meet with the Israelites" (v. 43), His chosen people. The particular verb used does not mean to meet casually or by accident but to meet deliberately, by appointment, by prearrangement. It is a verb not of coincidence but of rendezvous.

The Tabernacle is called, third, the "tabernacle of the Testimony" (38:21) or "Tent of the Testimony" (Num. 9:15). It served as the repository for the "ark of the Testimony" (Exod. 25:22), which held the "two tablets of the Testimony" (31:18) on which the Ten Commandments were inscribed. "Testimony" in such contexts is a technical term for the Ten Commandments themselves, the stipulations of the Mosaic covenant.[1]

Although those three names for the Tabernacle all emphasize God's immanence, its fourth name—which appears earliest in the text of Exodus—is "sanctuary" (25:8). Meaning literally "place of holiness," it stresses the transcendence, the otherness, the aloofness of God. Not only immanent (right here), God is also transcendent (out there). But though the Tabernacle is a sanctuary, the same verse that calls it that goes on immediately to say that the Lord will "dwell among" His people (v. 8). God lives not only "in a high and holy place, but also with him who is contrite and lowly in spirit" (Isa. 57:15).

●The appointment of Bezalel and Oholiab (31:1-11; 35:30—36:7)

The Tabernacle was to be built according to a prescribed pattern and detailed specifications (25:9, 40; 26:30; 27:8; 39:42-43). Although a large number of skilled and dedicated men and women would share in doing the work (35:10, 25-26), they would be supervised by Bezalel and his helper, Oholiab. All of the craftsmen possessed "skill" (31:6; literally "wisdom"), but it is said only of Bezalel that he was filled

1. See Kenneth A. Kitchen, *Ancient Orient and Old Testament* (Chicago: Inter-Varsity, 1966), pp. 108-9.

with the "Spirit of God" (31:3; 35:31). The supervisors' names are appropriate indeed, since Bezalel means "In the Shadow of God" and Oholiab means "[God] the Father Is My Tent." During the early stages of work on the Tabernacle the generosity of the people's giving had to be restrained because they had already brought more than enough materials to complete the task (36:4-7). Such liberality always results in divine blessing (Mal. 3:10).

The Courtyard (27:9-19; 38:9-20). The Tabernacle itself was a tentlike structure surrounded by a courtyard (38:20), the length of whose north and south sides was a hundred cubits each. Its east and west ends were each fifty cubits wide. Since a cubit equals about eighteen inches, the courtyard was about one hundred fifty feet long—half the length of a football field. As in the later Temples of Solomon and Zerubbabel, as well as in the Tabernacle itself, the courtyard entrance was on the east (27:13-15). Curtains five cubits high (27:18) and fastened at intervals to sturdy posts surrounded the entire courtyard, effectively shielding its activities from unauthorized public view.

Furnishings for the courtyard (27:1-8; 30:17-21; 38:1-8).

•The altar of burnt offering (27:1-8; 38:1-7)

The location of the bronze altar of burnt offering was probably at the center of the eastern half of the courtyard (see 40:29). Since it was made of wood (27:1) overlaid with bronze (v. 2) and was hollow (v. 8), it was probably packed with earth when in use to keep it from burning up. Its dimensions were five cubits square, matching those of an altar of earth from the Solomonic period excavated at Arad in southern Israel in 1967-68 (see also 20:24). The horns at the four corners of the courtyard altar (27:2) were not only smeared with blood during sacrificial ceremonies (29:12) but also served later as symbols of asylum for those accused of murder (1 Kings 1:50-53; 2:28). The first object seen by the worshiper as he entered the courtyard, the altar itself reminded him of the supreme necessity of atonement for sin.

•The basin for washing (30:17-21; 38:8)

Bronze mirrors were melted down to make the basin (38:8), which was located in the courtyard about halfway between the altar and the Tabernacle (30:18). It was therefore easily accessible to the priests whenever they needed to wash their hands and feet before entering the Tabernacle or approaching the altar (30:20-21; 40:30-32). Although the washing referred to was ritualistic in nature, the basin served as a perpetual reminder that God's people must always approach Him with "clean hands and a pure heart" (Ps. 24:3-4).

The Tabernacle proper (26:1-37; 36:8-38). The length of the Tabernacle was the same as that of the goat-hair curtains that covered it (thirty cubits; 26:7-8), and its height was the same as that of the wooden frames supporting the curtains (ten cubits; vv. 15-16). Its width was probably also ten cubits, since its far (west) end consisted of six frames (v. 22) each of which was "a cubit and a half wide" (v. 16)—plus the thickness of the side and corner (v. 23) frames. These dimensions tally well with the floor plan of Solomon's Temple, which was sixty cubits long and twenty wide (1 Kings 6:2)— exactly twice those of the Tabernacle, after which it was doubtless patterned.

Since Solomon's inner sanctuary (the Most Holy Place; 8:6) was twenty cubits square (6:20), the outer sanctuary was forty by twenty (the inner and outer sanctuaries of Ezekiel's Temple have precisely the same dimensions; Ezek. 41:2, 4). We note that the outer sanctuary (the Holy Place; 1 Kings 8:8) of the Temple was twice as long as the inner sanctuary, and so we are safe in assuming that the same proportions held for the

Tabernacle: The outer sanctuary was twenty by ten cubits, whereas the inner sanctuary was ten cubits square. The Tabernacle's Most Holy Place was therefore a perfect cube (see also 1 Kings 6:20), reminding us of the "Holy City, the new Jerusalem" (Rev. 21:2), in the book of Revelation (21:16).

The frames (Exod. 26:15-25) and crossbars (vv. 26-29) that formed the superstructure of the Tabernacle were covered over by four successive sets of curtains made of four progressively stronger materials: linen (vv. 1-6), goat hair (vv. 7-13), ram skins (v. 14), and hides of sea cows (v. 14). Two smaller linen curtains were made as well, one to "separate the Holy Place from the Most Holy Place" (v. 33) and the other to close "the entrance to the [entire] tent" (v. 36).

The Tabernacle entrance opened on the east end toward the basin and altar (40:30). The east end of the Tabernacle was probably along a north-south line that exactly bisected the courtyard. Since the Ark was inside the Most Holy Place (26:34), it stood in the very center of the west half of the courtyard, just as the altar of burnt offering stood in the very center of the east half. The two most important furnishings related to the Tabernacle therefore occupied the two most important positions in the courtyard.

The inner curtain that separated the Holy Place from the most Holy Place (vv. 31-35) was to be opened only by the high priest (Lev. 16:11-12), and even then only once a year (16:2, 34) on the Day of Atonement (16:29-30; 23:26-32). Herod's Temple had a similar curtain, which was "torn in two from top to bottom" (Matt. 27:51)—by God Himself—at the precise moment of Jesus' death. The cross of Christ made it possible for those who believe in Him to have direct access to the very presence of God. The torn curtain symbolizes our Lord's broken body (Heb. 10:20), which opened for us a new and living way and gave us "confidence to enter the Most Holy Place" (10:19) through His blood.

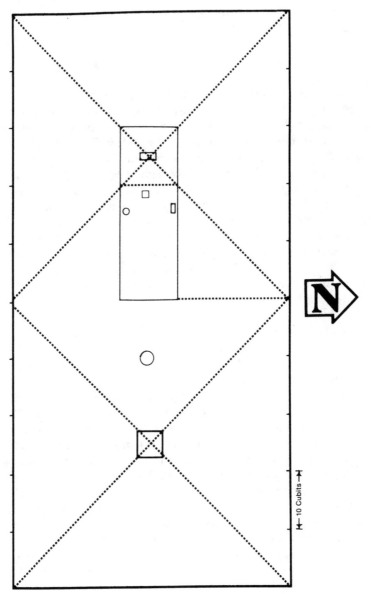

N

10 Cubits

Furnishings for the Holy Place (25:23-40; 27:20-21; 30:1-10, 22-38; 37:10-29).

•The table of the bread of the Presence (25:23-30; 37:10-16)

A small wooden table overlaid with gold (25:23-24) was to be placed outside the inner curtain "on the north side of the tabernacle" (26:35; 40:22). Every Sabbath day twelve fresh loaves of bread were to be set on the table in two rows, six in each row, as a lasting covenant before the Lord (Lev. 24:5-8). Later they would be eaten by the high priest and his sons as a part of their regular share of the offerings made to God (24:9). The number *twelve* symbolizes the participation of all the tribes of Israel—but only by proxy, since no one outside the priestly order was permitted to eat the bread of the Presence except in cases of extreme need (Matt. 12:4; Mark 2:26; Luke 6:4). The bread itself perhaps represents the Lord's provision of the basic necessities of life for His people (see Matt. 6:11; Luke 11:3).

•The lampstand and its oil (25:31-40; 27:20-21; 37:17-24)

"On the south side" of the Tabernacle (26:35; 40:24), outside the inner curtain and opposite the table, was a seventy-five-pound solid gold lampstand having a central shaft and six branches—"three on one side and three on the other" (25:32). Atop the shaft and each of the branches was a lamp (v. 37), possibly seven-spouted (such lamps have been found in archaeological excavations) and perhaps made of clay and therefore replaceable (although all the other accessories were made of pure gold; v. 39). The oil for the lamps was made of pressed olives and was to be kept burning all night throughout the year (27:20-21). The lampstand, or *menorah*, is a popular symbol of Judaism and of the modern nation of Israel. Spiritually it represents either God as a light to His people (see Num. 6:25) or Israel as a light to the Gentiles (Isa. 42:6; 60:3), whereas olive oil later symbolized the anointing power of the Holy Spirit (Zech. 4:2-6, 11-14).

•The altar of incense and the anointing oil (30:1-10, 22-38; 37:25-29)

Directly in front of the inner curtain that covered the entrance into the Most Holy Place was a small wooden altar overlaid with gold (30:1, 3, 6). Unlike the larger altar in the courtyard, the altar in the Holy Place was for the burning of incense, symbolic of the prayer and praise that ascends to God as a fragrant offering from His grateful people. The ingredients contained in the incense are listed in verses 34-35, and the altar itself was not to be used for any other kind of incense or offering (v. 9). Twice a day Aaron and his successors were to burn incense on the altar (vv. 7-8), and once a year on the Day of Atonement the horns of the incense altar were to be smeared with part of the blood of the sin offering (v. 10; see also Lev. 16:11-13).

Sacred anointing oil was also to be blended from various fragrant ingredients (Exod. 30:22-25). It was to be used to anoint the Tabernacle and its furnishings as well as the members of the Aaronic priesthood (vv. 26-31). As with the incense, so also with the anointing oil: On pain of death, no unauthorized use was to be made of it (vv. 32-33, 37-38).

The Ark (25:10-22; 37:1-9). The wooden chest overlaid inside and out with pure gold (25:10-11) and known commonly as the Ark was the only object that stood inside the Most Holy Place (26:33; 40:21). It functioned in three basic ways.

Called the "ark of the Testimony" (25:22) or "ark of the covenant" (Num. 10:33)—the two names are virtually synonymous—it served first of all as a repository for the two stone "tablets of the covenant" (Deut. 9:9) or "tablets of the Testimony" (Exod. 31:18)—that is, the tablets on which the Ten Commandments were written (Deut. 4:13; see Exod.

25:16, 21; 40:20; Deut. 10:1-5; 1 Kings 8:21). Also placed in
the Ark for safekeeping were a jar of manna (Exod. 16:33-34)
and Aaron's staff that had budded (Num. 17:10). All three
items—tablets, jar, and staff—are mentioned together in
Hebrews 9:4.

Second, the Ark was provided with "an atonement cover of
pure gold" (Exod. 25:17) that was sprinkled with blood once
a year on the Day of Atonement (Lev. 16:14) to symbolize the
forgiveness of sin and the appeasement of the wrath of God.

Third, two cherubim of hammered gold were made "of one
piece with the cover" (Exod. 25:19), symbolizing the presence
of God (Num. 10:35-36; 1 Sam. 4:3; 6:20) as well as His desire
to meet with His people (Exod. 25:22; 30:6; Josh. 7:6). The
cherubs were not the winged cupids of Renaissance art but
were the winged human-headed lions of ancient Mesopota-
mian and Syro-Palestinian art.[2] Cherubim served as armrests
or adorned the sides of royal thrones in the ancient Near East.
The Ark's cherubim, therefore, probably stood or crouched
parallel to each other, turning their heads to face each other
and spreading their wings upward over the intervening space
(Exod. 25:20). The Ark, then, was a symbolic throne for the
invisible God of Israel (1 Sam. 4:4), who held court between
the cherubim and ruled over His people as He met with them
there (Exod. 25:22).

We note in passing that the metals used in fashioning the
Tabernacle and its furnishings were more lustrous and costly
if they were near the presence of God in the Most Holy Place
than if they were farther away (for example, the furnishings
in the open courtyard were either made of or overlaid with
bronze, whereas those in the Tabernacle itself were either
made of or overlaid with gold).

The Typology of the Tabernacle. The Tabernacle and its
succeeding Temples, symbolizing as they did the desire of

---

2. William F. Albright, "What Were the Cherubim?" in *The Biblical Archaeologist Reader,* ed. G. Ernest Wright and David N. Freedman (Garden
   City, N.Y.: Doubleday, 1961), pp. 95-97.

God to dwell with His people, eventually came to typify God dwelling in Christ on the one hand and God (Father, Son, and Holy Spirit) dwelling with, among, and in Christians on the other. Jesus, for example, referred to His own body as a temple (John 2:19-21), in which "all the fullness of the Deity lives in bodily form" (Col. 2:9). Christians, individually and collectively, are called temples or houses in which the Holy Spirit lives (1 Cor. 6:19-20; Eph. 2:19-22; 1 Pet. 2:5). Such a relationship with God is made possible because Jesus "became flesh and lived for a while [literally, tabernacled] among us" (John 1:14). And some bright morning, when "the old order of things has passed away" (Rev. 21:4), all who believe in Christ will be able to say together, "Now the dwelling [literally, tabernacle] of God is with men, and he will live with them. They will be his people, and God himself will be with them and be their God" (21:3).

12

PRIESTHOOD

EXODUS 28:1—29:46; 39:1-31

Worship is the appropriate human response to divine redemption, and therefore the final sixteen chapters of Exodus concentrate on the Tabernacle (the place where God met with His chosen people) and the priesthood (the personnel especially designated to minister in it). As in chapter 11 we deviated slightly from the usual outline in order to bring together in one place and comment on all the Exodus material related to the Tabernacle, so we will do in this chapter with respect to all the Exodus material concerning the priesthood. It is hoped that this precedure will enable us to provide a clearer picture of the priestly office and its functions than would be possible otherwise.

2. *The priesthood: Its origin and purpose* (28:1—29:46; 39:1-31). Before a formal priesthood was established for the Israelites, elders and certain of the young men of Israel performed some of the duties (Exod. 24:1, 5) that would later become the responsibility of the officially appointed priests. Although in one sense it could be said that the entire nation of Israel was a "kingdom of priests" (19:6), it soon became abundantly clear that the tribe of Levi in general and the family of Aaron in particular would be consecrated by the Lord Himself to serve Him in a special way in that capacity.

Institution (28:1-2). The Aaronic priesthood is named after the first in its line, Moses' brother Aaron. From the outset it

124

was intended to be hereditary, including only Aaron's sons (v. 1) and their descendants (v. 43). The priesthood was a holy office, and "dignity and honor" were to be given both to Aaron (v. 2) and to his sons (v. 40). Such was only to be expected, since the Aaronic priesthood was instituted by God Himself.

Garments (28:3-43; 39:1-31). The pageantry and ritual of the priesthood, as described in the Bible, must have been impressive indeed—and the elaborate and beautiful garments worn by the priests doubtless contributed to the popular perception of the importance of the office as well as providing a fitting tribute to the majesty and glory of the Lord.

•General instructions (28:3-5; 39:1)

Bezalel and Oholiab, together with their associates, were to make the priestly garments. They were to use the various colors of linen that had gone into the fabrication of the Tabernacle curtains (39:1), but with a significant addition: Strands of pure gold (28:5), cut from thin sheets of the precious metal (39:3), were to be worked into the cloth from which the two main garments (ephod and breastpiece) were made. Presumably only Aaron (and his successors in the office of high priest) wore the ephod, breastpiece, robe, and turban, whereas it was primarily (though not exclusively) his sons who wore tunics, sashes, and headbands (28:40). Both high priest and lesser priests wore linen undergarments (vv. 42-43).

•The garments themselves (28:6-43; 39:2-31)

The high priest wore a loosely fitting apron or jacket called an *ephod* (28:6-14; 39:2-7). The front and back were fastened together by shoulder pieces at the top (v. 7) and held together by a waistband at the bottom (v. 8). Although later forms of the ephod resembled idols and were worshiped as false gods by backsliding Israelites (Judg. 8:27; 17:5; 18:14, 17-18, 20; see also Hos. 3:4), Aaron's ephod was a prominent feature of the high priestly garments and was made at the Lord's command (Exod. 39:5). Two specialties—those of the skilled craftsman and the embroiderer—were required for making the Tabernacle curtains (26:31, 36) as well as the priests' garments (28:6, 15; 28:39; 39:29), and a third—that of the weaver—became necessary as the work on the garments proceeded (39:22, 27).

Moses was commanded to have the names of the twelve sons of Israel, in the order of their birth (28:10; see Gen. 29:31-35; 30:4-13, 17-20, 22-24; 35:16-18), engraved on two onyx stones—six on one stone, six on the other. The two stones were then to be mounted in gold filigree settings and fastened on the shoulder pieces of the ephod. In that position the stones would remind the high priest of his responsibility to faithfully represent each of the tribes as he officiated in the services of the Tabernacle.

To the front of the ephod was attached a *breastpiece* (28:15-30; 39:8-21) made of the same material as the ephod (v. 15) and fastened to it with "braided chains of pure gold" (v. 22). The breastpiece was about nine inches square and was folded double (v. 16) to form a pouch. Mounted on the front of the breastpiece were four rows of precious stones, three in each row. Each of the stones was engraved with the name of one of the twelve sons of Israel.

It is fascinating to compare the kinds of stones listed here (vv. 17-20) with those that will decorate the foundations of the city walls in the new Jerusalem (Rev. 21:19-20). Just as the breastpiece stones bear the names of the twelve tribes of Israel, so will the foundations of the new Jerusalem bear the names of "the twelve apostles of the Lamb" (Rev. 21:14). Although the two lists are not identical, in each case the precise identification of a few of the stones is uncertain. Further research will perhaps clarify the nature of one or more of the unknown stones and possibly bring the two lists into closer correspondence with each other.

The purpose of the breastpiece was "for making decisions" (v. 15). The Urim and Thummim, deposited in the pouch, were sacred lots used as the "means of making decisions" (v. 30). The word "Urim" begins with the first letter of the Hebrew alphabet and "Thummim" begins with the last letter, so the lots were probably restricted to giving either positive or negative responses to questions asked of them. Strengthening that likelihood is the fact that the phrase "Urim and Thummim" is best translated into English as "curses and perfections," meaning that if "Urim" dominated when the lots were cast the answer would be no but if "Thummim" dominated the answer would be yes. Unfortunately we do not know how many lots there were, what they looked like, or exactly how they were used in actual practice. Numerous instances of consulting the Lord by means of them are recorded in the Old Testament, although the phrase "Urim and Thummim" is not always explicitly employed in such cases.[1] The casting of lots by an Israelite high priest was by no means the same as throwing dice, because the results were not determined by chance. The priest knew that the lots' "every decision" was "from the LORD" (Prov. 16:33). The last mention of a divine decision mediated through lots in the Bible is found in Acts 1:23-26. When the Holy Spirit came in power on the day of Pentecost (Acts 2:1-4), the need for the casting of lots disappeared.

Three times we are told that the breastpiece and its contents were "over his [Aaron's] heart" (Exod. 28:29-30). In that position the precious stones adorning the breastpiece would remind the high priest of his obligation to sympathize with the

---

1. See especially John Howard Raven, *The History of the Religion of Israel* (1933; reprint ed., Grand Rapids: Baker, 1979), pp. 85-86.

needs of each of the twelve tribes as he sought to discern God's will for them.[2]

A weaver (39:22) made for the high priest a blue *robe* that was worn under the ephod and that was somewhat longer than it (28:31-35; 39:22-26). Varicolored cloth pomegranates alternating with gold bells were attached to the hem of the robe. A popular Jewish interpretation of 28:35 taught that one end of a long rope should be tied to the high priest's ankle before he entered the Holy Place. Since his slightest movement would cause the bells to tinkle, the people outside would assume that all was well as long as they could hear them. But if the bells fell silent for a time, the people outside would naturally assume that their priest had either fainted or died. They would then tug on their end of the rope to pull him out, making it unnecessary for unauthorized persons to enter the Holy Place in order to remove his body.

The phrase "HOLY TO THE LORD" (v. 36) was engraved on a *plate of pure gold*, which in turn was attached to the front of the turban worn by the high priest (28:36-38; 39:30-31). It was a "sacred diadem" (39:30) to remind Aaron and the Israelites that their sacrifices and gifts were always to be brought to the Lord in the proper way and with the proper motivation. God's people should always be holy in all that they are and do.

The *turban* to which the plate was attached was worn only by the high priest, whereas the *tunics, sashes,* and *headbands* were more specifically (though not exclusively) for the lesser priests (28:39-41; 39:27-29). In both cases the garments sym-

---

2. Although the breastpiece and its contents were handed down from generation to generation, they probably did not survive the destruction of Jerusalem in 586 B.C. Jewish historians say that a second breastpiece was made for Zerubbabel's Temple late in the sixth century B.C., but it too was lost when the Romans under Crassus ransacked the Temple in 54 B.C. and took all its treasures. A unique modern replica of Aaron's breastpiece, made in accord with the biblical instructions, is on permanent exhibit in the Roger Williams Inn at the American Baptist Assembly conference grounds in Green Lake, Wisconsin.

bolized the "dignity and honor" that was due to all who occupied the priestly office (vv. 2, 40).

All the priests wore linen *undergarments* "reaching from the waist to the thigh" (28:42). Their purpose was to preserve the modesty of the priests while they were engaged in performing their duties (v. 43), especially (in later years) when they ascended steps leading up to altars (Ezek. 43:17; see also Lev. 9:22).

Consecration (29:1-46). After Aaron and his sons had put on their newly made garments, Moses was to anoint and ordain them as priests in a service of consecration (28:41; 29:7-9)—a solemn service described not only in Exodus 29 but also in Leviticus 8.

•Steps in the sacrificial process (29:1-26)

One of the most important aspects of the ordination ceremony was the series of sacrifices offered in connection with it. Since the procedure followed gives us an excellent impression of how Old Testament sacrifices were brought to the Lord on other occasions as well, it will be helpful to comment briefly on the process of blood sacrifice as described here.[3]

Exodus 29:1-9 describes the *selection of the sacrificial animals.* The bull and two rams chosen were to be "young" and "without defect" (v. 1). They were to be the best the offerer had—in the prime of life and showing no visible scars or blemishes. Since God never asks His people to do anything that He is unwilling to do Himself, He offered to us His one and only Son, Jesus Christ—in the prime of life and "without blemish or defect" (1 Pet. 1:19). (Every step in the Old Testament sacrificial process typifies the perfect sacrifice of Christ Himself).

At that point in the ordination ceremony, bread, cakes, and

3. See Ronald Youngblood, *The Heart of the Old Testament* (Grand Rapids: Baker, 1971), pp. 81-85, for additional details.

wafers were also brought (vv. 2-3), and Aaron and his sons were washed with water (v. 4), clothed in their priestly regalia, and anointed with oil (Aaron immediately, his sons somewhat later; see v. 21).

A laying on of hands is commanded in Exodus 29:10, 15, 19. At three separate junctures in the service of ordination, the priests laid their hands on the heads of each of the animals, in this case symbolizing the transfer of sin from the offerer to the sacrifice (see especially Lev. 16:21-22). Similarly, Jesus "bore our sins in his body on the tree, so that we might die to sins and live for righteousness" (1 Pet. 2:24). When God the Father laid our sins on God the Son, the ultimate fulfillment of Isaiah 53:6 was realized (as the apostle Peter clearly understood; see 1 Pet. 2:24-25).

Though described very briefly, *putting the animal to death* was the central and most important act in the sacrificial process (29:11, 16*a*, 17, 20*a*). The Hebrew word translated "altar" (in v. 12, for example) means literally "place of slaughter," and the location of the bronze altar in the center of the eastern half of the Tabernacle courtyard made it the focus of attention when sacrificial offerings were brought to the Lord. Similarly, a cross became the altar on which Jesus died (Phil. 2:8) "for our sins" (1 Cor. 15:3), substituting Himself for us just as animals had earlier been substituted by offerers for themselves or for others (see especially Gen. 22:13). That the cross is central to the New Testament proclamation of salvation is clear from Paul's testimony: "I resolved to know nothing while I was with you except Jesus Christ and him crucified" (1 Cor. 2:2; see also Gal. 6:14).

"The life of a creature is in the blood, and I have given it to you to make atonement for yourselves on the altar; it is the blood that makes atonement for one's life" (Lev. 17:11). The blood that secures atonement symbolizes both propitiation (appeasing the wrath of God) and expiation (forgiving and removing the sins of God's people). *The blood applied* to the altar represented God's acceptance of the priestly sacrifice (29:12, 16*b*, 20*b*-21). Willingness to hear and obey was symbolized by the application of blood to the lobes of the right ears of Aaron and his sons. Putting blood on the thumbs of their right hands and on the big toes of their right feet symbolized readiness and ability to serve (just as cutting off thumbs and big toes symbolized the effective removal of those qualities; see Judg. 1:6-7).

All who believe in the Lord Jesus are saved (Acts 16:31)—not because of what we have done but because His blood "purifies us from every sin" (1 John 1:7). Indeed, "he is the atoning sacrifice for our sins, and not only for ours but also for the sins of the whole world" (1 John 2:2; see also Rom. 3:25).

Whether as a sin offering (v. 14) or as a burnt offering (v. 18), certain *parts of the slaughtered animal were to be burned* (29:13-14, 18, 22-26). Those that were presented as a burnt offering on the altar are described as emitting "a pleasing aroma" to the Lord (vv. 18, 25)—obviously a burning not of destruction but of sublimation into something finer and more acceptable than it was before. Sacrifice involves consecration and dedication as well as propitiation and expiation.

Jesus' death "freed us from our sins by his blood" (Rev. 1:5), but it also represented an act of consecration on His part. Christ "gave himself up for us as a fragrant offering and sacrifice to God" (Eph. 5:2). Although we ourselves will never be able to die for another person in an expiatory sense, we can—in response to all that Jesus has done for us—offer our bodies "as living sacrifices, holy and pleasing to God" (Rom. 12:1). Such is the very least that we should be willing to give to God's dear Son, who is at one and the same time our great High Priest and our sacrifice (Heb. 4:14—5:10; 6:19—7:28; 8:3; 9:1-28; 10:10, 14, 21-22; see also 1 Tim. 2:5).

•Additional regulations (29:27-37)

Included here are instructions concerning the parts of the ordination ram that Aaron and his sons were given as food (vv. 27-28, 31-34). We learn also that every time a new high priest was ordained in the future he was to wear Aaron's sacred garments, which were to be passed down from generation to generation (vv. 29-30). The first ordination service was to set the pattern for all such future services: it was to be seven days in length (vv. 35-37; see also v. 30).

•Initial priestly duties (29:38-46)

For Aaron and his sons, as for God's ministers through the ages, ordination and consecration led immediately to service. The priests were to officiate daily at the altar by sacrificing to the Lord two burnt offerings—one in the morning and the other at twilight (vv. 38-42*a*; for additional details see Num. 28:3-8). The Lord Himself promised to meet with and speak with His people on every such occasion (vv. 42*b*-43).

The concluding paragraph of Exodus 29 summarizes God's intention to consecrate Aaron and his sons to serve Him as priests (v. 44) and reaffirms His earlier promise to dwell among His people (see 25:8) and be their God (see 6:7). Verse 46 ties together priesthood and covenant by using the language of the preamble ("I am the LORD your God") and historical prologue ("who brought you out of Egypt") that had already served to introduce the covenant stipulations known as the Ten Commandments (see 20:2).

13

RENEWAL

Exodus 32:1—34:35; 39:32—40:38

Sandwiched between the chapters that give the Lord's instructions for making the Tabernacle and the priestly garments on the one hand (Exod. 25:1—31:18) and the sections that outline the actual manufacture of the Tabernacle and garments on the other (35:1—39:31) are three chapters that tell about Israel's first major violation of the Sinaitic covenant and about what happened as a result (32:1—34:35). The book of Exodus then ends with a majestic description of how the finished Tabernacle was dedicated (39:32—40:38). Since 32:1—34:35 and 39:32—40:38 both fall under the general heading of renewal, we have grouped them together to form the final chapter of this volume. In so doing we are deviating only slightly from the outline given at the end of the first chapter.

3. *Covenant breach and renewal* (32:1—34:35).

The Golden Calf (32:1-10). After the ratification of the Sinaitic covenant, Moses went up on the mountain for a period of time that would last forty days and nights (24:18). The Israelites grew tired of waiting for him, so they asked his brother, Aaron, to make them one or more "gods" (the Hebrew word *elohim*, although plural in form, may be translated either as a singular or a plural; see also vv. 4, 8, 23, 31) to replace Moses as their leader (v. 1). Although it was the Lord Himself who had brought them up out of Egypt (20:2), the people gave the credit to Moses. Now that he was gone they decided that they needed someone (or something) else to guide them.

Aaron responded to their demands by casting a gold idol in the shape of a calf and using a special tool for its detailed features (vv. 2-4). The calf was probably intended to represent one or more manifestations of the Egyptian bull-god Apis (later called Serapis). Unusually fine specimens of bulls were deified and worshiped by the Egyptians in ancient times. When such bulls died they were embalmed and then secreted in an underground mausoleum known as the Serapeum, which can be seen by visitors to Egypt even today.

Some of the Israelites had earlier worshiped false gods in Egypt (Josh. 24:14). After the Lord gave His people the Ten Commandments, however, they no longer had any excuse for continuing in idolatry. They were neither to make nor worship an idol in the form of anything on earth (Exod. 20:4-5), and they were told specifically not to make "gods of gold" (20:23) since to do so was to commit a "great sin" (32:31). Firmly declaring that they would obey God and Him alone (19:8; 24:3, 7), they nevertheless turned their backs on Him to worship idols. Worse still, they blasphemed God's name by claiming that neither the Lord nor Moses had brought them up out of Egypt but that the calf had done so (32:4).

"These are your gods, O Israel, who brought you up out of Egypt" (v. 4). Centuries later the Israelite king Jeroboam I would say the same thing as he introduced idolatry into the Northern Kingdom through the worship of two golden calves that he made (1 Kings 12:28). Jeroboam also announced a festival in connection with the calf worship (12:32), a procedure similar to that of Aaron (Exod. 32:5). It is not surprising that after they sacrificed offerings to Aaron's calf, the people began to "indulge in revelry" (v. 6), because throughout biblical times idolatry was frequently carried on in connection with all kinds of immorality (Gal. 5:19-21; 1 Pet. 4:3) and could even be used as a synonym for other sins (Col. 3:5). Since the Sinaitic covenant had now been broken, God in speaking to Moses referred to the Israelites as "your people" (v. 7) and "these people" (v. 9), no longer willing or able to call them "my people" as He had done before (3:7; 6:7). They were now a "stiff-necked people" (v. 9), stubbornly refusing to obey God, who declared His intention to destroy them and begin His elective purposes all over again by making Moses the ancestor of a "great nation" (v. 10). Aaron's sinful compliance with the people's wishes, meanwhile, would be remembered by both Stephen (Acts 7:39-41) and Paul (1 Cor. 10:6-7) as an example of willful disobedience.

Moses the Intercessor (32:11—33:23). Moses, like Abraham before him (Gen. 18:23-33) and Amos after him (Amos 7:2, 5), prayed earnestly for the Israelites and used the phrase "your people" as he spoke to God on their behalf (v. 11). Moses felt free to ask the Lord to relent on the basis of the earlier covenant He had made with Abraham, Isaac, and Jacob (v. 13; see, for example, Gen. 22:15-17). Paul argued as follows in a similar situation: "As far as election is concerned, [the Israelites] are loved on account of the patriarchs, for God's gifts and his call are irrevocable" (Rom. 11:28-29).

"The prayer of a righteous man is powerful and effective" (James 5:16), and Moses was just such a man. The Lord "relented" (v. 14; see also Amos 7:3, 6)—not because His nature or character had changed but in order to honor (even if only temporarily and partially) the fervent prayer of His righteous servant.

Moses then descended the mountain, carrying the "two tablets of the Testimony" (v. 15; see 31:18 and especially 25:22). Each of them was "inscribed on both sides, front and back" (v. 15), and each doubtless contained all ten of the covenant stipulations (the Ten Commandments). In ancient times two copies of every suzerainty treaty (one for the suzerain, one for the vassal) were always made, and each copy contained the text of the entire treaty. We assume therefore that each of the two stone tablets of the Testimony contained the entire Decalogue. One of the copies belonged to the covenant-making God (the Suzerain), the other to His covenant people, Israel (the vassals)—but both were deposited in the "ark of the Testimony" (25:22; see 25:16). The tablets had been written by God Himself (v. 16; 31:18), making the people's sin against the second Commandment (20:4-6) all the more reprehensible.

Part of the way down the mountain Moses met his young aide, Joshua (v. 17; see 24:13), who thought he heard the sound of war in the camp below. It turned out, however, to be the sounds of the kind of singing (v. 18) and dancing (v. 19) that could only be due to "running wild" (v. 25). When Moses arrived in the camp he smashed the tablets (which had already been figuratively broken by the people in any case) in righteous indignation. He then burned the golden calf, ground it to powder, threw it into the people's water supply, and made them drink it. The purpose of the latter act is unknown, but it is ironic that the remnants of the golden calf were now consumed by the very people who had earlier offered sacrifices to it (v. 6).

Aaron's excuses were as desperate as they were lame (vv. 22-24), and Moses was not fooled by them. He recognized the fact that Aaron had allowed the people to get out of control and become a potential laughingstock to their enemies (v. 25). Obviously not all of the people were guilty, but those who were had to be punished. The Levites, Moses' tribal relatives (2:1-2; 6:19-20), volunteered to be one of the instruments of divine judgment (vv. 26-28). As a reward for their willingness to undertake so difficult and tragic an assignment they were set apart to the Lord (v. 29) and were later made responsible for the care of the Tabernacle (Num. 1:50-53; for a similar incident see Num. 25:6-13). The other means used by God to judge the people who had worshiped the golden calf was a plague (v. 35).

Moses' continued intercession for his people did not gloss over their sin, but his great love for them made him willing to do anything to secure God's forgiveness for them. He even pleaded with the Lord to blot him out of the divine register, the book listing the names of heaven's citizens (see also Rev. 20:15; 21:27), if that was the only way his people could be saved (v. 32). Paul's similar readiness to be separated from God's presence forever for the sake of his Israelite kinsmen (Rom. 9:3-4) was perhaps inspired by Moses' remarkably selfless statement.

But the Lord replied to Moses by telling him that each sinner must die for his own sin (v. 33)—an emphasis that became especially strong in the writings of the prophets who ministered during the final years of the Southern Kingdom (see, for example, Jer. 31:30; Ezek. 18:1-32). Moses was still God's choice to lead the people to the Promised Land (v. 34), though they continued to be stiff-necked and stubborn (33:3). Apparently to keep them from melting down their jewelry to make another idol, the Lord told them to strip off their ornaments (33:4-6). God sometimes uses drastic measures to keep His people from falling into temptation.

Chapter 33 adds to the strong impression given by the book of Exodus that Moses enjoyed an unusually intimate relationship with God. The Lord had earlier assured Moses of His personal presence (3:12) and power (4:15-17), so Moses was doubtless surprised when God stated that He would not continue to go with him (33:3) but would provide His angel as a guide instead (32:24; 33:2). But Moses was understandably reluctant to proceed on his journey with his people until he received some kind of guarantee of the Lord's presence. So he went to the "tent of meeting" (not the Tabernacle, which had not yet been made; this particular tent was pitched outside the camp) to ask the Lord for His renewed favor and blessing (33:7-9, 12-13). The story of their conversation clearly indicates that the fellowship between God and Moses was profound indeed.

The pillar of cloud would come down and stay at the entrance to the tent whenever Moses went inside (vv. 9-10).

Since the presence of the Lord was in the pillar (13:21), Moses could feel confident that God would not forsake him.

In the tent the Lord would speak to Moses face to face (v. 11). The expression is not to be taken literally, since we are also told that Moses was not allowed to see the face of God (vv. 20, 23). Speaking face to face here means, rather, "as a man speaks with his friend" (v. 11)—that is, openly and cordially. In Numbers 12:8, where we read that God spoke with Moses "face to face" (literally, "mouth to mouth"), the expression is immediately explained to mean "clearly and not in riddles"—that is, not in a hidden or secret way.

The Lord knew Moses by name (vv. 12, 17), an expression that again stresses the intimacy of their relationship (since "name" in the Bible implies "essence" or "character").

Moses had found favor with God (vv. 12-13, 16-17), an expression used in the Bible only with respect to God's choicest servants (see for example Gen. 6:8). God had made Moses the object of His special concern and loving care. He had bestowed unmerited grace on him.

The Lord responded graciously to another of Moses' bold and daring prayers (vv. 12-17). By promising that His Presence would go with Moses and the people, God was in effect promising to renew His covenant with them. Moses' faithfulness to the Lord had brought blessing to the people as well.

Then Moses, emboldened even further, asked God for one more thing: a vision of His glory (v. 18). The vision would remain tantalizing and mysterious and partial, consisting of God's "goodness" (v. 19) and His "back" (v. 23), but the Lord nevertheless answered this prayer of Moses as well. Even the afterglow of God's glory must have been a remarkable sight to behold.

Especially significant is the proclamation of the name *Yahweh* given here: "I will have mercy on whom I will have mercy, and I will have compassion on whom I will have compassion" (v. 19). The positive and gracious emphasis intended in God's statement is further clarified in Romans 9:16, where Paul (after quoting Exod. 34:19 in Rom. 9:15) affirms that God's saving relationship to His people does not "depend on man's desire or effort, but on God's mercy." Moses could do nothing whatever to gain even a minimal glimpse of the glory of God. Such an experience could occur only through grace.

Moses' unique relationship to God as detailed in Exodus 33 is beautifully summarized in Deuteronomy 34:10-12, where among other things we are told that "no prophet has risen in Israel like Moses, whom the LORD knew face to face" (Deut. 34:10). No other figure is paid such a high compliment in the Old Testament. Moses was indeed a spiritual giant.

The New Stone Tablets (34:1-35).

•A gracious God proclaims His name (34:1-9)

Since the first set of tablets had been broken (32:19), and since the covenant was about to be renewed in accordance with God's promise (33:14), the Lord commanded Moses to chisel out "two stone tablets like the first ones" (v. 1). Moses proceeded to do so and then repeated the earlier procedure of going up Mount Sinai (v. 4) and staying there forty days and forty nights (v. 28). While he was there the Lord gave him yet another revelation of the meaning of *Yahweh.*

Part of the description of God's nature found in verses 6-7 is repeated from 20:5-6, where the Israelites were commanded not to make idols—a warning that they needed to hear again in the light of the golden calf incident. Exodus 34:6-7, whose phrases are quoted in whole or in part throughout the rest of Israel's history in the Old Testament (Num. 14:18; Neh. 9:17; Pss. 86:15; 103:8; 145:8; Joel 2:13; Jonah 4:2), contains both positive and negative emphases concerning the name and nature of God.

Negatively, God "does not leave the guilty unpunished; He punishes the children and their children for the sin of the fathers to the third and fourth generation." Other people, and especially our children, are affected harmfully by the sins we commit. When we sin we destroy ourselves and others, and for those sins God holds us responsible and declares us guilty.

Positively, the Lord is "the compassionate and gracious God, slow to anger, abounding in love and faithfulness, maintaining love to thousands, and forgiving wickedness, rebellion and sin." The love mentioned twice in this sentence is more specifically God's covenant love, a relationship that God bears toward His people when He chooses them for Himself. Although the results of sin extended only to the third and fourth generation, the covenant love of our faithful God has continued "to thousands" of generations (see 20:6; Deut. 7:9; 1 Chron. 16:15; Ps. 105:8). When we reciprocate His covenant love, the Lord responds by forgiving our "wickedness, rebellion and sin"—the three main terms used in the Old Testament to describe disobedience toward God. "Wickedness" is literally the "bending" or "twisting" of God's will and purpose, "rebellion" is open revolt against God's commands, and "sin" (by far the most common term) is "missing the mark," or goal, that God has set for us.[1]

• A faithful God renews His covenant (34:10-28)

Periodic renewals of the Sinaitic covenant were necessary throughout Israelite history (see Deut. 5:2-3; 29:1; Josh. 24:25; 2 Kings 23:1-27), and the first of them had to take place soon after the golden calf incident. It is therefore understandable that strong emphasis was placed on the wickedness of the sin of idolatry. Israel was to break down pagan altars, smash "sacred stones" (probably representing

---

1. For an alternate (though related) way of understanding the same three terms see Ronald Youngblood, "A New Look at Three Old Testament Roots for 'Sin,' " in *Biblical and Near Eastern Studies,* ed. Gary A. Tuttle (Grand Rapids: Eerdmans, 1978), pp. 201-5.

male deities) and cut down "Asherah poles" (symbols of the Canaanite goddess Asherah). One of God's names is "Jealous" (v. 14), meaning that He brooks no rivals and is zealous for His uniqueness and holiness. Political alliance and intermarriage with Canaan's inhabitants was forbidden—not because of lack of neighborliness or for ethnic or racial reasons but because such relationships would inevitably involve acceptance of Canaanite pagan worship (vv. 15-16). Stress was therefore given to the proper observance of the three main annual festivals of Israel's religious calendar (vv. 18-24), an emphasis that appeared earlier in the Book of the Covenant (23:14-17).

Other related matters (vv. 19-20*a*, 21, 25-26) are interspersed with the festival regulations and are also quoted from previous sections of Exodus (see 13:12-13; 20:9-10; 23:18-19). Moses was commanded to record all these words in writing once again (v. 27), as he had done with the more extensive Book of the Covenant earlier (24:4). The Lord Himself rewrote the Ten Commandments (v. 28) as He had promised He would (v. 1) and as He had inscribed the original tablets in the first place (31:18).

•A loving God honors His servant (34:29-35)

When Moses came down from the mountain the second time, the reflected glory of God radiated from his face. Moses found it necessary to keep his face veiled to avoid frightening the Israelites, and he removed the veil only when he entered the "tent of meeting" to speak with the Lord. The only exception to that practice was whenever he read aloud to the people any of the Lord's newly given commands (vv. 31-32). Paul compares this account with the infinitely greater glory that accompanies the ministry of the new covenant through the Holy Spirit (1 Cor. 3:7-18).

4. *Dedicating the Tabernacle* (39:32—40:38). The book of Exodus concludes with a solemn ceremony of dedication and

consecration of the Tabernacle and priesthood. Moses inspected all the work done on the Tabernacle and its appurtenances (39:32-43), received the Lord's command to set up the Tabernacle and to anoint it and the priests (40:1-16), and proceeded to obey that command (vv. 17-33). Only one event was yet to occur before Israel's elaborate system of worship could begin with all of its impressive pageantry and profound symbolism.

That element is mentioned twice in the final section of Exodus (40:34-38): "The glory of the LORD filled the tabernacle." Although Moses had earlier said to the Lord, "Show me your glory" (33:18), even he "could not enter the Tent of Meeting" (v. 35) because the sight of God's glory within was so overwhelming and awe-inspiring.

Some day, however, Moses would see the glory of God in all its fullness—or, rather, in all *His* fullness. Moses and Elijah appeared on the Mount of Transfiguration with the radiant Christ and spoke with Him about His "departure" (Luke 9:31)—EXODOS in the Greek text of the New Testament. Moses had led his people in an exodus from Egypt, and now—nearly fifteen hundred years later—he was talking about a second exodus, which Jesus would make from this world. Sharing that moment of revelation on the mountain through sleep-filled eyes were three of Jesus' disciples, who, when they looked at Jesus, "saw his glory" (9:32) along with the two men standing there. Needless to say, Moses saw that glory also—and his centuries-long wait had been supremely worthwhile.

For Moses, faith had finally become sight.

BIBLIOGRAPHY

Cole, Robert Alan. *Exodus: An Introduction and Commentary.* Downers Grove, Ill.: Inter-Varsity, 1973.

Cox, Leo G. *Exodus.* Beacon Bible Commentary. Vol. 1. Kansas City, Mo.: Beacon Hill, 1966.

Davis, John J. *Moses and the Gods of Egypt.* Grand Rapids: Baker, 1971.

Huey, F. B. *Exodus: A Study Guide Commentary.* Grand Rapids: Zondervan, 1977.

Johnson, Philip C. "Exodus." In *Wycliffe Bible Commentary.* Edited by Charles F. Pfeiffer and Everett F. Harrison. Chicago: Moody, 1962.

Keil, C. F., and Delitzsch, F. *The Pentateuch.* Biblical Commentary on the Old Testament. Vols. 1-2. Reprint. Grand Rapids: Eerdmans, 1959.

Kitchen, Kenneth A. *Ancient Orient and Old Testament.* Chicago: Inter-Varsity, 1966.

Knight, George A. *Theology as Narration: A Commentary on the Book of Exodus.* Grand Rapids: Eerdmans, 1977.

Pfeiffer, Charles F. *Egypt and the Exodus.* Grand Rapids: Baker, 1964.

Ramm, Bernard. *His Way out.* Glendale, Calif.: Gospel Light, 1974.

Unger, Merrill F. *Unger's Bible Dictionary.* Chicago: Moody, 1957.

Vos, Howard F. *Archaeology in Bible Lands.* Chicago: Moody, 1977.

Wallace, Ronald S. *The Ten Commandments.* Grand Rapids: Eerdmans, 1965.

Wiseman, D. J. "Law and Order in Old Testament Times." *Vox Evangelica* 7 (1973).

Youngblood, Ronald. *The Heart of the Old Testament.* Grand Rapids: Baker, 1971.

———. "A New Look at Three Old Testament Roots for 'Sin.' " In *Biblical and Near Eastern Studies.* Edited by Gary A. Tuttle. Grand Rapids: Eerdmans, 1978.

Youngblood, Ronald. "A New Occurrence of the Divine Name 'I AM.' " *Journal of the Evangelical Theological Society* 15 (1972).

Moody Press, a ministry of the Moody Bible Institute, is designed for education, evangelization, and edification. If we may assist you in knowing more about Christ and the Christian life, please write us without obligation: Moody Press, c/o MLM, Chicago, Illinois 60610.